THE SOLO CHEF

First published in 2014 by
New Holland Publishers Pty Ltd
London • Sydney • Cape Town • Auckland

The Chandlery Unit 114 50 Westminster Bridge Road London SE1 7QY
Wembley Square First Floor Solan Road Gardens Cape Town 8001 South Africa
1/66 Gibbes Street Chatswood NSW 2067 Australia
218 Lake Road Northcote Auckland New Zealand

www.newhollandpublishers.com

A record of this book is held at the British Library and National Library of Australia

ISBN 9781742573991

Managing director: Fiona Schultz
Publisher: Patsy Rowe
Designer: Tracy Loughlin
Editor: Simona Hill
Proofreader: Meryl Potter
Stylist: Tracy Rutherford except pages 45, 51, 84, 93, 112 stylist Julio Castellano.
Photographers: Andy Lewis pages 45, 51, 84, 93, 112, NHIL pages 4, 7, 10, 19, 23, 114, 137, 169.
All other photos Sue Stubbs
Production director: Olga Dementiev
Printer: Toppan Leefung Printing Ltd (China)

10 9 8 7 6 5 4 3 2 1

Keep up with New Holland Publishers on Facebook
www.facebook.com/NewHollandPublishers

THE SOLO CHEF

cooking for one is easy

Catherine Baker

With recipes by Diana Ferguson

NH
NEW
HOLLAND

Dedication

This book is dedicated to our parents who
gave us a love of good food;
a gift that keeps on giving.

CONTENTS

INTRODUCTION

The advantages of living by yourself are numerous and almost too obvious to cite: complete control of the TV remote, guilt-free consumption of the last piece of chocolate, wearing underpants around the living room, best of all, the knowledge that you can just have cheese on toast for dinner, night after night.

Now, if you are in complete agreement with that last point then this book is probably not for you. Just put it back down and head off to the deli for a wedge of Pecorino and a wheel of Brie. No hard feelings and bon appétit!

If, on the other hand, you'd agree that cheese on toast, albeit virtuous in its simplicity, not to mention its cheesiness, does have its limitations, then read on.

Currently in most western countries, anywhere between 20 and 30 per cent of all households are single, and the numbers are on the rise. They are estimated to grow by another 10 to 15 per cent by the mid 2020s. So, for those of you out there living and cooking by yourselves, you are definitely not alone in doing so. Neither would you be alone in thinking that cooking just for yourself is a chore. After years of running 'Cooking for One' workshops throughout the community, we've discovered that most solo chefs feel that cooking for themselves is repetitive, wasteful, seemingly futile, and, well, repetitive.

Knowing the statistics, it's always struck us as odd that practically all cookbooks and food magazines are designed for families and present recipes that cater for four or even six people. Those publications simply don't provide solutions for the one in four households in which people live by themselves and where, ironically, the challenges of cooking for one can be greater than cooking for a family.

There are a multitude of reasons why you may find yourself cooking solo: perhaps you've just moved out of home for the first time, or perhaps someone has moved out of yours. Maybe you live with a shift-worker, a plain old fussy-eater or someone whose needs are different to yours (or maybe you're the fussy eater!). For some of you the person or people that you loved cooking for are simply no longer around, and that can be challenging in itself. The reasons why people are cooking alone are as varied as the individuals, but the challenges they face are often the same and this book offers solutions to the main ones.

As you read through this book, hopefully you will see that there is hope, and that your kitchen need not be limited to a microwave and a toaster. You will also see that the recipes are all quick and simple to follow because, while there may be some proficient solo chefs out there who know how to make the perfect soufflé, when you are cooking just for you, most of the time you want something that is delicious to eat, but no-fuss to make. The ingredients are everyday items which are easy to purchase and use. The dishes are tasty and nutritious.

It's a cookbook, yes, but more than that. We recognise that solo chefs need motivation and understanding, and this book has oodles of both. Hopefully it will give you the inspiration you need to make a few simple changes to your cooking routine, so that your overall lifestyle changes for the better.

THE CHALLENGES OF COOKING FOR ONE

Our Cooking for One workshops have shown us what the main issues are that single people face when planning, shopping and cooking for themselves. They are:

• Lack of motivation or 'I can't be bothered' syndrome
• Cooking for one is wasteful or 'slimy crisper drawer condition'
• Eating leftovers is boring, or 'repetitive meal malaise'
• Portion control—'one extra spoonful won't hurt, will it?'
• Avoiding processed foods—'ready meals anonymous'

If you've been cooking for yourself for a while, then the problems that we've identified here may strike you as being familiar. But don't worry - you aren't the only one feeling unmotivated, wasteful, bored, overfed and yet empty all at once. Almost everyone we have met over the years has had the same experience, because they've all been faced with exactly the same hurdles to overcome. Let's look at each challenge in a little more detail and see what can be done about them.

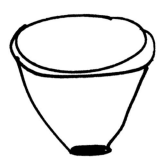

'I can't be bothered' Syndrome

Lack of Motivation

It's the perennial question: 'Can I be bothered to cook for myself when I could just have cheese on toast for dinner (again)?' The question is a legitimate one, and, frankly, it's not going to go away. You may ask yourself this question every day, so it's important to understand what it is that's stopping you from wanting to cook in the first place.

People often say it's hard to find the motivation to cook just for themselves and generally don't want to spend an hour in the kitchen preparing a meal just for one. Why not? Well, how much time have you got? There probably isn't enough room in this book to delve into all of the anthropological, not to mention psychological, reasons why people aren't as motivated to cook for one as they are to cook for several. Is it because of a lack of self-worth? Perhaps for some. Is it down to a lack of affirmation, with no-one to coo over your dish? For others this is certainly true. Or is it a lethargy that kicks in only when you know you can get away with it? For many, absolutely. All of these reasons, and many others, are valid ones to feel unmotivated. But if you are feeling a certain sluggishness on your way to the kitchen each evening, can we at least say this: you ARE worth it! Coo over your own dish!

Secondly, people complain that they don't have time to cook. Then they say that they definitely don't want to have to wash up multiple pots and pans just for one; and finally, they never have the right ingredients in the store cupboard. Many despair at the sight of a cupboard full of food but which somehow contains nothing to eat. Sound familiar?

Our Solution

So, motivation is whittled away by three main culprits: time, cleaning and lack of ingredients. In this section we will address the first two, and ingredients will be looked at later on. But let's just say this: all of our recipes are quick to make, easy to clean-up afterwards and use a variety of ingredients and cuisine types to help you stay inspired and enthusiastic about your cooking.

To help minimise your time in the kitchen almost all of the recipes we've included are designed to have you in and out of the kitchen in less than 30 minutes, and in many cases less than half that time.

To find the quickest and easiest recipes, check the time guide for each recipe. On nights where you can spare the extra few minutes, try some of the longer recipes, but don't feel like you have to every single night. The main thing is to enjoy the process of cooking and eating your meal.

Cleaning: Many of the recipes here are 'one-pot recipes', which make cleaning up afterwards quick and easy. Others use a sheet of foil or baking paper in the oven instead of a baking tray and that's it! No cleaning at all. Again, check the recipes that are a 'one-pot dish'.

Other dishes in the book make use of leftovers in innovative and interesting ways, so that

half the cooking has already been done. This can be a major time and energy saver, too. There is an entire section dedicated to making and using leftovers. Once again, use the guide on each recipe to see which ones suit you best.

Finally, if you are a bit of an Old Mother Hubbard, with nothing in the cupboard to eat, then you'll find a list of must-have store-cupboard ingredients a little further on in the book. A well-stocked cupboard containing the right ingredients will ensure that you always have something tasty, nutritious and quick to put on the table. They are ingredients which are versatile and easy to use and they feature time and time again in the recipes here so you have plenty of inspiration to use them.

So, if you are feeling unmotivated, there are solutions at hand. Making dinner need not be a chore, especially when you have a range of recipes that will leave you plenty of time to sit in front of the telly with your feet up in not much more than half an hour.

Slimy Salad Drawer Condition

Cooking for One is Wasteful

The waste challenge is a biggie. No doubt you've perused the fruit and vegetable aisle at your supermarket countless times, and have been so enthused by the thought of a whole creamy-white cauliflower, or a seductively crispy iceberg lettuce that you've been misguided enough to actually purchase it, only to find it looking like a science experiment in the bottom of the refrigerator about eight days later.

Most singles find that supermarkets don't cater for their needs. Often meat, fruit, vegetables, and even bread are packaged for the family shopper, and so the single person's preferred aisle somehow becomes the one that contains the canned soup. Some supermarkets are getting better at providing food packaged for the single shopper, but not all of them, so it's useful to know how you should shop in order to avoid being a wasteful cook. Reducing excess makes sense from an economic point of view, but if you need another reason, then avoiding waste also helps our environment, too.

Our Solution

The first and most effective solution to the whole waste issue is making sure that you purchase versatile ingredients that can be used in a range of dishes. This will help to ensure that you use the entire quantity of what you buy.

For example, buying a bag of baby spinach leaves is a better idea than buying a whole lettuce, because spinach leaves can be used in both cooked and raw dishes, making them twice as useful. They can also be prepared really quickly—literally grab a handful of them, hold them under a running tap and voilà! There is no chopping to contend with. They wilt down in cooked dishes in a matter of seconds, adding texture, colour, and vitamins and minerals in the easiest way. No iceberg can do all that.

A second solution to waste is to be realistic, and instead of buying all fresh and highly perishable vegetables, purchase a mix of fresh, canned and frozen ones so that you always have something quick and easy to prepare, no matter when you last did the shopping.

Also, try to make meals throughout the week that use the same ingredients but in different ways, to ensure you use all of what you buy. To help you with this, you'll find recipes in this book where there are many ingredient items that come up again and again. These are the ones listed in the list of Super Single Ingredients on page 17 and we recommend that you include as many of them as you can on your own shopping list.

Yet another solution to waste—and we hate to mention this for fear of losing some of you at this point—is learning to be organised. Your best friend in this regard? The freezer. Using your freezer effectively means that your food dollar will go as far as it possibly can.

There is a whole section on how to use your freezer effectively, but for now, make sure that you get into the habit of doing the following:

Separate meats into single portions as soon as you get home from the supermarket and freeze them individually (see page 14 for a guide to what is a reasonably sized single portion). Use purpose-made freezer bags and/or layers of freezer paper to do this cleanly and efficiently.

If you make a double or triple quantity of a dish (and invariably you will for dishes such as curries, spaghetti sauces and casseroles), portion out the leftovers when you are plating up your meal and freeze them as soon as they are cold. Don't wait to do this three days later when the dish is at its most unappetising.

Repetitive Meal Malaise

Eating Leftovers is Boring

Over the years almost every piece of advice we have come across about cooking for one sprouts the same 'revolutionary' idea: make large quantities of a dish and then freeze the leftovers for subsequent meals throughout the week. We don't have to tell you how boring and disheartening this uncreative approach appears to be to most solo chefs. It's paraded around like a panacea for single cooks, when really it can be the source of significant angst.

Having said that, from time to time you are going to cook up large quantities of some dishes. Dare we say it, but sometimes you will actually feel like making a large meal. You are therefore going to be faced with leftovers and the nagging issue of what to do with them so that you don't have to eat the same meal time after time.

Our Solution

We suggest multiple and creative uses for leftovers. We've dedicated an entire section to this subject, so check each recipe's guide as to what dishes use which leftovers. For 'large quantity' recipes we have indicated the number of portions that each makes so that you know just how many dishes you can make from one batch. For example, the Bolognese sauce recipe makes enough for four portions. So have spaghetti with your sauce once or even twice, but reinvent the remaining portions to become something else, such as a shepherd's pie, or a delicious savoury turnover or enjoy with nachos or a hearty jacket potato instead.

A bag of fresh coleslaw mix (without the dressing) is a terrific purchase from the supermarket. It takes all of the fuss out of preparing vegetables for a coleslaw. Yet the size of most of those bags is too much for just one person, and who wants to eat coleslaw all week? A better idea is to use some of it for a deliciously crunchy and fresh coleslaw, then, use the rest in a stir-fry. Still got some left over? Use it again as a side dish of vegetables, steamed with a little butter and lemon juice.

The point is that most people see leftovers as just that: something that is left over from a previous meal, when instead if you change your thinking you'll start seeing them as a starting point for your next meal. Perception is everything! They are ingredients, not remainders, so experiment with them.

One Extra Spoonful Won't Hurt Will It?

Portion Control

How much is enough? How much is too much? The answer to what is a correct portion is usually found somewhere on a fine and notoriously slippery line. There are various culprits— the Extra Dollop, the Generous Serve, and, the worst offender: the Second Helping. They show up on our plates night after night. Whether your large portions are the result of culinary over-zealousness or just plain greediness, portion control is a problem for many single cooks. But let's not dwell on it. We all know what we are doing. The questions is, what can we do about it?

Our Solution

We are not going to profess that we have the solution to every single person's diet. These days it's hard to know whether you should be cutting out sugars or fats, or both. It's not clear either if you should only be doing this at certain times during the day, because at other times it's apparently OK. But then according to some people it's only OK if you don't eat carbohydrate and protein in the same meal, because that's not OK either. OK?

In any case, we are both a little bit old school and believe that a diet of moderation (a little bit of everything and a lot of some things, like vegetables) combined with exercise is a good thing for keeping us healthy. But that's because it works for us. For other people that we know, cutting out all sugars (including carbs) has provided them with long-term success in managing their weight. When it comes to diet, different things work for different people, so ultimately you need to find what works for you.

What we can do is ensure that the recipes in this book are based on reasonable portion sizes for one person. Here is a rough guide:

The portions in this book per single serving are:
- poultry, meat and fish, 125–150 g (4–5 oz)
- processed meats, such as bacon, 50–75 g (2–3 oz)
- rice, couscous and pasta, about 1 cup cooked quantity:
    ⅔ cup (60 g/2¼ oz) uncooked pasta will produce 1 cup (145 g/5 oz) cooked
    ⅓ cup (70 g/2¾ oz) uncooked rice will produce 1 cup (180 g/6¼ oz) cooked and
    ⅓ cup (60 g/2¼ oz) uncooked couscous will produce 1 cup (130 g/4½ oz) cooked
- pastry, half a pre-made sheet (100 g/3¾ oz)
- potatoes, two or three small chat potatoes or 1 medium-sized potato

For other vegetables, don't feel restricted by the quantity indicated in the recipes here, although we would not be using less than what is stipulated. It's important to get as many vegetables into your diet as possible, so in this area we would encourage you to add more and experiment with new ones wherever possible. That's why almost all of the recipes here have a list of 'extra optional ingredients' which you can experiment with, and more often than not these are extra vegetables.

As a cautionary note, many nutritionists now recommend eating red meat no more than three or four times a week, and that you limit your consumption of processed meats. We certainly wouldn't recommend eating processed meats such as bacon or ham every night of the week and you probably wouldn't want to eat them that often, but for the occasional quick and easy meal they are fabulous.

Top tips for portion control

Try to have a little discipline when plating up. If you have cooked more than one serving of a meal, then it's always better to serve the 'spare helping' first, putting the food in a storage container, before serving up your current meal.

For ingredients such as meat, make sure that you divide them into single portions as soon as you get home from the supermarket and freeze them as single serves. This will not only save on defrosting time, but will ensure that you don't overeat at meal times, or feel obliged to eat the same ingredients several evenings running.

Check out Using your Freezer Effectively on page 29 for more information on how to use your freezer to best effect.

Cuts of meat that freeze beautifully as individual portions include:

- Steaks (fish and beef varieties)
- Chops
- Sausages
- Chicken breasts and tenderloins
- Lamb shanks
- Rissoles
- Schnitzels
- Chicken Marylands

Ready Meals Anonymous

Avoiding Processed Foods

There is no disputing that there are plenty of ready meals available for those who dine regularly by themselves, as well as for families. Quick macaroni and cheese, frozen roast dinners, vacuum-packed curry and rice, chilli beef in a tin, noodle cups, single-serve lasagne, and—the staple of every single person's pantry—cans of soup. With so much variety, boredom is not the problem with the choice of ready meals available. And neither is it convenience. There's no denying that it's far easier to just 'zap' something in the microwave for a couple of minutes and have dinner steaming on the table before you can say 'nutritional value', than it is to cook from scratch. So, what is the problem with this kind of meal?

Nothing, if it's an occasional thing. There's definitely a time and place for ready meals, and that goes for family chefs as well as solo ones. The problem with meals where all the fuss is taken out of their preparation is that invariably there has been quite a lot of 'fuss' put into their ingredients. Highly processed foods such as ready meals tend to contain a lot of sugar, salt and preservatives, not to mention artificial additives. And, in our experience, many people (rightly) want to avoid eating foods that contain large quantities of these.

The other 'problem' with regularly eating ready meals and take-away dishes is that you end up not cooking anything at all. And, in a somewhat contradictory predicament, many people cooking for one don't want to spend too much time in the kitchen, but they do actually want to cook for themselves instead of outsourcing it all to a supermarket or the local take-away. There is enjoyment and even some kind of therapy to be had in cooking, and not doing any at all can be depressing.

Finally, there is another problem with ready meals, and that is that they are—almost always—unsatisfying to eat. You can find yourself scrounging around the plastic dish for the last soggy grain of rice or waterlogged cube of carrot in a futile attempt to feel full. Home-cooked food fills you up more and leaves you feeling sated, a sensation often under-rated by many, yet absolutely key to feeling good about your food.

Our Solution

The fact that you are using this book to cook at all means that you are not reaching for an all-in-one ready-made meal at least some of the time, which is a good thing. By putting together your own meal you are cooking your ingredients from scratch, rather than just reheating something that has already been cooked in a factory.

If you are in a ready-made meal rut, then start off slow, and aim to make just one or two meals per week for yourself. You will find that after a while you will start to enjoy not just the better tasting, fresher food, but also the time in the kitchen, and, we kid you not, a stronger feeling of self-respect because you have 'bothered' to cook for yourself.

WHAT TO BUY AND HOW TO SHOP

These days there are an abundance of cookbooks that assume you've got a thousand different staples in your cupboard. We don't especially want to join them or preach to people about what they should have in their fridges and pantries. However, we would like to point out that there are some everyday ingredients you can buy that are particularly useful when cooking for one, and they (and their virtues) are listed on the following pages. They've made it on to the list either because of their size, which means they are the perfect portion for one person; their versatility, which means you are more likely to use them; their storage qualities and packaging characteristics, which mean that they last a little longer; or because, quite simply, they are brilliant, no-fuss ingredients. Granted, some of them may cost a little more at the check-out, but if it means that it's destined for your dinner rather than your rubbish bin two weeks later, then you'll probably agree that it's worth it. Remember, there are economies in avoiding waste.

Super Single Ingredients

Butter
Using real butter in your cooking adds flavour and richness to everyday meals. It can transform dishes in ways that oil and margarine simply cannot. Using a little here and there will definitely delight your tastebuds and make you more inclined to enjoy what you've cooked (remember it's all about motivation). Keep a pack of it refrigerated; it will last for weeks if kept cold.

Carrots
They will last for up to three weeks in the crisper (salad) drawer of the refrigerator. They are versatile and can be used cooked or raw. Carrots are easily portioned and stored for one person. And, best of all, they are a great healthy ingredient to add to your meals or to use for snacking.

New (Chat) Potatoes
These little apples of the earth are wonderful because they don't require peeling, and that's something which might make you that little bit more inclined to actually have potatoes with your dinner. (Having said that, did you know that it takes about 45 seconds to wash, peel and

chop a potato?) New potatoes are easy to portion accurately for one person. They are great steamed as a side vegetable, or chopped up and added to a dish as an ingredient. They work beautifully with mayonnaise as an instant serve of potato salad.

Jacket (Baked) Potatoes (Red-skinned)
These potatoes are terrific because they don't require peeling, though they may need a quick wash. They are easily cooked in the microwave or baked and very little preparation is required. The skin provides a great source of fibre and is good for you. Serve as a side dish with a dollop of sour cream.

Cherry Tomatoes
Their smaller size means that you can portion them accurately for one person. You can also banish the dreaded leftover half-tomato that stares up at you from the fridge. Because cherry tomatoes require less or even no chopping, you may be more inclined to use them. They are great raw in salads or cooked in pasta and gnocchi dishes. They also make a fabulous healthy snack.

Couscous
Couscous is the 'forgotten carb' in the sense that it's a wonderful alternative to rice, pasta and potatoes, mainly because it adds variety, but also because it's quicker and easier to prepare than any of the other three. Basically, if you can boil a kettle, you can cook couscous. Couscous has a very subtle flavor of its own, so it is incredibly versatile and can take on the other flavours of your dish. It is great in hot and cold dishes, and complements curries and spiced food particularly well. It also responds well to being dressed, like a salad, with a vinaigrette. All-up it's a great way to make many meals just a little more filling.

Eggs
Eggs will last for about four weeks, which means you have plenty of time to work your way through a dozen, adding them into different hot and cold recipes. They can be a whole meal in themselves or an added ingredient. Eggs are good for you and are a cheap source of protein. They also take almost no time to cook, so the idea of them is encouraging in itself.

French Eschalots
Not to be confused with spring onions (scallions) or shallots, these have been our secret weapon in the kitchen for so many reasons. Firstly, their smaller size means that you use a whole one each time, avoiding the 'half onion in the fridge' scenario. Secondly, their flavour is sweeter than that of their larger brown and white friends—more like a Spanish onion, which means they can be used cooked or raw, making you more likely to use them. They are wonderful as a base in stews and casseroles, or accompanying salads, and in sauces for steaks and other meats. Try roasting them whole, too.

Gnocchi

Gnocchi are small potato dumplings that you buy ready-made and cook as you would pasta in boiling water. The great thing about gnocchi is that they cook in next to no time (usually less than 2 minutes). They are great as a side dish with a little butter and cheese—no need to even make a sauce.

Ready-made Frozen Pastry

Many people tend to forget that pastry is an alternative 'carbohydrate'. They labour under the misconception that pastry is fiddly and difficult to work with. But, in reality, ready-made pastry is an absolute dream to cook with. It is quick and easy to use and it gives that lovely baked quality to your meal (so many meals for one are stove-top produced, your oven can feel a bit like an elephant in the room, so it's great to finally bake something for yourself). Pastry is used in several of the recipes here—take a look at our 3 different pizzas for some ideas to get you started.

Prepared Mixed Vegetables

Preparing vegetables often puts people off cooking anything at all, but when the peeling and chopping is done for you, there's no excuse. One of the quickest and easiest ways to add more vegetables to your diet is to throw a generous handful of ready-prepared vegetables into whatever you are cooking (Bolognese sauce, curries, stir fries, soups, etc.). This can be fresh vegetables such as coleslaw mix or frozen such as peas, carrots and corn mixes. When using the frozen variety you often don't need to defrost them first, just add them and continue cooking for a few minutes until they are done. They will also cook easily in the microwave or in some simmering water for a couple of minutes for an easy side dish. Need another reason? Many nutritionists believe that frozen vegetables actually retain their vitamins and minerals better than fresh vegetables because they are frozen quite quickly after they are picked.

Lemons and Lemon Juice

Having a constant supply of lemons in your kitchen is always a good idea. Lemon juice can be used to add a quick and easy dressing to salads, to add a lovely tang to many 'saucy' dishes, to freshen the flavour of steamed vegetables, and as an easy marinade for meats.

Baby Spinach or Rocket Leaves

These leaves are easily the most versatile ingredient in your fridge. Once again they can be used cooked or raw, making them twice as likely to be consumed. They are so easy to prepare for salads. And they will wilt down in hot dishes in a matter of seconds. A handful of them can be added to sandwiches, burgers and salads, to top pizzas, into soups, casseroles and stir fries, or simply added in with other steamed vegetables. And they are so good for you.

Baby Cos Lettuce

If you're not a fan of baby spinach leaves but you still want to enjoy the crunch of something 'salad-y', then another great option is to buy baby cos (romaine) and mini baby cos lettuces. They are far more nutritionally useful than iceberg lettuces, and because they are small and tightly furled, you will find that you can unwrap just a couple of layers at a time for a meal, and then return the rest to the fridge for use on another day. Try not to cut your lettuce with a knife if you intend to return it to the fridge as this is what causes it to discolour and turn brown. Baby cos is probably not as useful in cooked meals as baby spinach, but it is great for salads.

Ready-made Stock

Stock is the key to many simple, tasty and nutritious recipes, but many of us can't be bothered to make our own. Good, flavoursome ready-made versions that contain natural ingredients are widely available, and we would encourage you to buy these, and their salt-reduced cousins wherever possible.

Stock can be purchased in small quantities such as 375 ml (13 fl oz) and 500 ml (17 fl oz), which helps to avoid waste. However, sometimes even these are too much for one person, so freeze any left over in ice cube trays, and then next time you need just a little bit, simply add a couple of frozen cubes. Crumbling a small amount of a stock cube into a dish also helps to add flavour, so a ready supply of these is a good idea, too.

Small Tins of Tuna, Salmon or Crabmeat

These are great to have in the pantry and will keep for months, even years. They are good for salads and lighter meals and are an easy alternative to red meat. Their small size is just right for one person, too.

Small Tins of Vegetables

It's important to have a good mix of fresh, frozen and tinned vegetables in store so that no matter when you last shopped, you have some ingredients at the ready. Beans and pulses, such as chickpeas (garbanzo beans), lentils, borlotti beans, kidney beans or mixed beans, as well as corn kernels and diced peeled tomatoes lend themselves well to canning, but there are others that are good too. They are versatile for salads as well as cooked dishes, and can often be substituted for meat in a meal—see Spicy Red Beans (page 108) The smaller cans are great for reducing waste.

Smoked or Cured Meats

There may be days where you haven't thought ahead in the morning to what you'll be having for dinner. Not to worry. Even if you've just got a packet of luncheon meat of some kind, you can still pull together a meal. Many of the recipes in this book use smoked or cured meat such as ham, bacon, shaved or sliced cooked chicken or turkey breast, smoked salmon or ocean trout, for precisely this reason. These meats last longer when refrigerated than fresh meats, and, with new packaging, many brands are now often portioned for individual consumption, which means less waste. They are wonderful in salads and cooked dishes, so you will be more likely to work your way through them, no matter what food mood you are in.

Snack Boxes of Sultanas (Golden Raisins)

Not just a lunch-box item. Little boxes of sultanas are the perfect portion for one person and work in so many different dishes. We use them in Coleslaw, Lamb Curry, and Bread and Butter Pudding. They are indeed great as a snack, too.

Dairy Products

These consist of small packets of grated (shredded) mixed cheese, squares of processed cheese, some grated (shredded) Parmesan cheese, or marinated cheeses such as feta and goat's cheese in oil, and sour cream. Being on your own, you don't always get through a whole block of cheese before the tell-tale greenish signs of neglect start to appear around its edges. Having a more versatile supply of cheese is a better option. And by versatile we mean small bags of already grated mixed cheese. Grated cheese has all the work taken out of it for cooking, and tastes just as good in sandwiches. A mixed cheese content (for example mozzarella, tasty (cheddar) and parmesan) is also great because it means you can add it to pizzas for topping without fear of burning, or to spicy dishes for added flavour.

A jar of grated (shredded) parmesan cheese is also great to have on hand for pasta dishes. A sprinkle will add extra bite and flavour to the most simple dishes, and it will last for ages when refrigerated.

What can also be useful to have on hand is a supply of individual portioned processed cheese squares, which are great to spread on toast and sandwiches, but which will also melt down in pasta sauces and other dishes to add depth of flavour and a velvety-smooth consistency. They last for up to 12 months in the fridge if still in their foil wrapper so they will definitely not go to waste.

Still on cheese, if you prefer a more gourmet option, then splurge on a jar of marinated goat's or feta cheese in oil (sometimes they come with herbs, too). These are just fabulous as a snack on crackers, but also on pizzas, salads, or omelettes. Because of the oil marinade they will last a lot longer in your fridge than classic versions.

Finally, the other dairy product that we simply can't do without is sour cream. It finds its way into so many of the recipes here, if only as an optional ingredient, because it simply tastes great both in and on dishes. The light versions are good, too, so feel free to use those if you prefer.

Squeeze Bottle of Pizza Base Sauce

This is a great alternative to buying tubs of tomato paste (purée) that you only ever seem to use half of. It's not quite as thick and concentrated as tomato paste so it works wonderfully as the base of a pasta sauce, not to mention actually using it as a pizza base on small pita breads or pastry sheets for individual pizzas. It is so versatile and keeps refrigerated for up to a month even after opening.

Must-have Condiments

Mayonnaise, Dijon Mustard, Seedy Mustard
Firstly, we will just say that all of these are so much more than just sandwich condiments. They can be useful in the kitchen for salad dressings and side 'dipping' sauces.

Mayonnaise can liven up freshly steamed vegetables, and can be a simple 'sauce' to go with meats such as schnitzel and fish. Try mixing it with a squeeze of lemon juice and a dash of cayenne pepper.

Both Dijon and seedy mustards are superb with steak, and can be turned into something positively divine when mixed with a little sour cream in a pan that has just cooked your steak.

Try combining them with a little mayonnaise and a couple of cooked chat potatoes for an instant gourmet potato salad.

Salt and Pepper
For salt we tend to use the good old-fashioned table variety, and for pepper a 'four peppercorn blend' in a disposable grinder. Both are easy to find in your local supermarket.

Oil for Cooking
Light olive oil is a versatile cooking oil that is very popular and works perfectly for all of the dishes in the book, though a plain blended vegetable oil will do just as well. We've put light olive oil in all of the recipes for this reason. If you are buying olive oil, you may be tempted to buy extra virgin oil perhaps thinking it isbetter quality than the light version. It is superior for some things, but not really to cook with (it addes great flavor to salads and when drizzled over cooked food) so it's fine to just buy a plain light olive oil for general all-purpose use.

Tabasco or Chilli Flakes
For added heat, we recommend keeping either of these to hand, as they are both easily added to dishes while cooking.

Cumin
If we had to choose just one spice for our kitchen, it would definitely be cumin. It works to add a curry hint to many dishes, but can also form the basis of Tex-Mex and Moroccan flavours as well. It will add spice to meat and delicious flavour to mince. It adds depth of flavour to vegetables and sides dishes such as couscous, too.

Alcohol

We usually have an open bottle of wine in the house, and find adding a splash of red or white to a dish very easy and not in the least bit wasteful. However, if you don't regularly have wine open, then the opposite can be true—opening a whole bottle just for a dash of it is a waste. If you enjoy the flavour benefits of adding alcohol to food but don't want to be driven to drink for the sake of a good sauce, then there are alternatives. In place of white wine try using vermouth (which lasts in the drinks cabinet just like a sherry or port) and for red wine you can, in many cases, replace it with a little cooking brandy, which also lasts a long time on the shelf (depending on your drinking habits, of course).

THE RIGHT TOOLS FOR THE SOLO CHEF

If you haven't forked out for the latest celebrity chef-endorsed cooking knives or don't have a state-of-the-art non-stick frying pan, then our advice to you would be—don't!

Having the right tools is important in the kitchen, particularly if they are going to save you time and effort. This is doubly so when you are cooking for one and if motivation is pretty thin on the ground. But don't let a lack of fancy utensils put you off because, at the end of the day, the main thing is just to get into the kitchen and start cooking.

Firstly, we have compiled a list of the small equipment items that are particularly helpful when you are cooking for one, mainly because they will save you time and elbow grease. Some of them just help you to be a little bit more organised, and others will help with portion control. Most are everyday items and none of them need to be particularly expensive.

Then, after that, we've gone into quite a bit of detail about how to use two of the bigger items that solo chefs find useful—the freezer and the microwave—so you can really make them work for you in the kitchen.

List of Tools and Equipment

Vegetable Steaming Device

You could use a Chinese steaming basket, saucepan steamer, rice cooker/vegetable steamer machine or a microwave. Steaming is the best and easiest way to cook vegetables to retain flavour, colour and nutrients; however, a side dish of vegetables is quite often the thing that you simply can't be bothered preparing to make a 'complete' meal. So, set yourself up to be motivated by having an easy way to cook vegetables. You may find that having just the one, small microwave dish that you use and clean each night is the way to go. Others may like to leave their rice cooker/steamer permanently sitting on the bench so that they actually use it. Whatever the solution is for you, once you've found it, cooking vegetables for dinner won't seem such a chore.

Non-stick Frying Pan and Saucepans

Non-stick surfaces require less fat when cooking, and will be less likely to burn your food. What's not to love about that? These days you can get good non-stick saucepans and frying pans from your local supermarket for little cost, and, granted, they probably won't last a lifetime, but at that price, they can easily be renewed when they become a little worse for wear.

The important thing to note with pots and pans is to get the right size for one person. A 30 cm (12 in) frying pan is too big, and will persuade you to cook too much. A 15-20 cm (6-8 in) size is perfect for single servings, and indeed for all of the frying pan recipes in this book.

For saucepans, we recommend having three—the most important ones being one small and one medium. A large one is fine to have for big batches of cooking, but you'll probably hardly ever need it for everyday meals.

Cooking and Storage Containers

It's worth a trip to a good kitchenware store to invest in cooking containers that are the right size for one person. Buy your kitchenware according to your cooking needs rather than cooking a large quantity just to fill the container. Don't buy classic size meatloaf tins when you can easily find cute little ones that are perfect for one or two servings. Stock up on individual ramekins and pie dishes (many of the recipes here use an 8 or 10 cm [3 or 4 in] diameter ramekin). Buy microwave and storage containers that will lend themselves to individual portions. The extra dollars you spend in setting yourself up will be worth it when you reduce waste.

Colander or Sieve

Many of our recipes involve draining foods that have been cooked in hot water. It's much safer and easier to do this using a colander or a sieve. They can be found quite cheaply at your local supermarket.

Kitchen Knives

Contrary to popular belief, sharp knives are actually safer to use than blunt ones, because you won't have to exert Viking force on, for example, an unassuming chat potato, and find your hand slipping in the process and resulting in thumb salad. Basically, sharp knives will save you elbow grease and time.

Good quality knives can be expensive, so initially treat yourself to just one special all-purpose knife. For your other chopping needs, settle for something less fancy, but do invest in a good knife sharpener.

Mixing Bowls

Some of us have as many as 12 mixing bowls in our kitchen when the reality is that we only ever seem to use the same two. Yep, two good quality glass mixing bowls will usually suffice for even the most ardent cooks. One small and one medium-sized can be used to make salads, mix recipe ingredients, microwave vegetables and even as serving dishes if the occasion calls for it.

Measuring Cups and Spoons

These are cheap and useful when following recipes. Getting into a habit of using them regularly will help with portion control. Buy a couple of sets and keep the right-size cup in your rice and pasta containers so you can easily measure out the correct quantity for one serving each time.

Hand-held Blender or Liquidiser

These little electric friends are so useful for a quick mashed potato, soup or purée. They often come with other fixtures, such as a whisk or blender bowl ,which makes them truly multipurpose.

Flat Baking Sheet or Tray

This book has several recipes that require a flat baking tray to be used with a sheet of baking paper or foil. You can get a good one from your local supermarket.

Wraps and Baking Aids

This includes items such as plastic freezer bags, ziplock bags, foil, baking paper, clingwrap or freezer paper. Take the time to check out this section of your supermarket. You will be amazed at the storage inventions that exist and so much of it is useful for the single cook.

Refer to the section on freezing for more information on how to use some of these items effectively.

Other utensils that are a must:
• Wooden or plastic spoons and spatulas that won't damage non-stick surfaces.
• Vegetable peeler.
• Can and bottle opener.
• Potato masher.
• A garlic press. Simply put a whole unpeeled clove of garlic in and press firmly. No need for peeling or chopping.
• A couple of plastic chopping boards. They are inexpensive and easy to clean. You can get colour-coded sets so that each board is used for a particular item such as meat, seafood, vegetables.

Using Your Freezer Effectively

Earlier we mentioned that the freezer can be a trusted friend in the kitchen. It can really help you to make the most of your weekly shop. Having said that, it's important to know that not everything freezes well. Dishes that contain a lot of dairy products, such as cream, for example, don't freeze well. So, set yourself up for success by trying to freeze only things that lend themselves to the freezing process.

The key to freezing anything successfully is to ensure the product has minimal contact with air when it is in the freezer. Invest in some good quality freezer bags, freezer wrap, foil and containers, and keep your precious goodies wrapped tightly against the cold.

The longer anything stays in the freezer, the lesser the quality will be upon defrosting, so try not to freeze anything for longer than three months.

Freezing is a very drying process, so if you are freezing cooked dishes, then extra liquid and moisture added during the cooking process will help to ensure that it defrosts well.

Freezing Vegetables

If you know you are just not going to eat those carrots or that celery before it's too late, you can try freezing them. Home-frozen vegetables don't last as long as their store-bought counterparts (probably only three to four weeks) because the home-freezing technique is not as efficient as the industrial one, but it's still worth the effort.

However, you can't just pop them in the freezer willy-nilly. In almost all instances you will need to chop and blanch them first (i.e. cook them in boiling water for a short period, from a few seconds to a few minutes). As a rough guide:

- For softer vegetables, such as leeks and spinach, chop up and blanch for 30–60 seconds before draining and freezing in freezer bags.
- For root vegetables such as carrot, potato and onion, blanch for 2–3 minutes.

Freezing Herbs

For 'soft' herbs such as parsley, mint, chives and dill, wash by soaking in a sink or bowl of cold water, and letting any grit or sediment sink to the bottom, and then finely chop. Half-fill an ice cube tray with water, then place a couple of teaspoons of the chopped herb into each 'cube' before freezing. This method of freezing herbs preserves the herbs for use in cooking, but not for garnishing a dish. Basil does not freeze well.

For 'twiggy' herbs such as rosemary and thyme, wash, dry and then place the sprigs in a freezer bag and just pull a sprig or two out when required.

Portion Out Meats Before Freezing

When freezing meats, it's a great idea to portion them into single servings (such as 150 g, or 5 oz diced beef, two or three chicken tenderloins, two sausages) for freezing. Ziplock freezer bags are great for this. Or invest in some freezer paper and wrap individual serves in paper before layering several in a plastic container in the freezer. Then simply take out a single serve to defrost. You will save on defrosting time and it will help your portion control, too.

Freezing Liquids

For lemons, simply squeeze their juice and freeze in ice cube trays.

For leftover stock, also use an ice cube tray or even small ziplock bags for small amounts.

Final Word on Freezing

This book is packed with recipes that do freeze well. In fact, all of the 'multiple portion' dishes will freeze beautifully, allowing you to save those extra portions for another day and for use in another dish. Some examples—to get your mouth watering—are Bolognese sauce, Spicy Red Beans and delicious French-style Lentils.

FOODS THAT FREEZE WELL

Soups and stews

Raw egg whites

Cooked lasagne and cannelloni

Gravy

Uncooked meat or mince and poultry

Bread

Mashed potato and other mashed root vegetables

Cooked rice can be frozen and reheated again using a little water

Some vegetables and herbs

FOODS THAT DON'T FREEZE WELL

Creamy sauces and creamy soups

Emulsion sauces made using butter or oil (for example, vinaigrettes, béarnaise sauce or mayonnaise)

Dishes containing gelatine, or which have used a lot of flour or cornflour (cornstarch) for thickening

Cooked pasta (except in lasagne or cannelloni) will turn to mush when frozen and reheated

Vegetables, fruits and herbs with a very high water content, such as raw lettuce, cabbage, cucumber, strawberries, melon, and basil, which blackens when over-chilled.

Using Your Microwave Effectively

We know there are some people out there who are, quite simply, opposed to using a microwave, and if that is the case for you, then just ignore this particular paragraph of advice. The microwave is a great piece of equipment for heating leftovers without fear of burning them, which is great if you eat them on a regular basis. Having said that, we find that their real virtue is in cooking vegetables in a quick and easy way.

Microwaving Vegetables Successfully

Some of our recipes require you to cook vegetables. If, like others, you find preparing vegetables for one a chore, this method of cooking may suit you.

Microwaves provide the quickest and easiest way of getting vegetables on the table. All you need is a glass bowl and some cling film (plastic wrap) or a microwave dish with a lid, some water and some salt.

It's important to point out that all microwaves are different, and you may find that with yours, these times are either over-, or under-cooking your vegetables. It is a process of trial and error, but once you have found the perfect time setting for each one, you will just keep using it night after night, and it will make 'difficult vegetables' a thing of the past.

For green vegetables, such as broccoli, beans, snowpeas (mange tout) and zucchini (courgette) rinse the vegetables, trim and chop, where required, then place into the small glass bowl, add a little water, cover and add a pinch of salt. Microwave on high for 3 minutes and they are perfect to eat.

Corn on the cob: rinse and place into a glass bowl with a little water and cover. Microwave on high for 6 minutes.

Other root vegetables, such as carrot, pumpkin and sweet potato: peel and dice, and place in a glass bowl with a little water to cover. Add a pinch of salt. Microwave on high for 5 minutes.

Jacket potatoes: cut a 'cross' into one side of the skin, then place in a glass bowl, add a little water and cover. Microwave on high for 6 minutes. Remove from the bowl, place into a baking dish and into the oven (180°C/350°F/Gas mark 4) for 15–20 minutes, or until turning crispy.

Chat potatoes: rinse and place into a glass bowl with a little water to cover. Add a pinch of salt. For three or four chats, microwave on high for 4 minutes.

Microwaves never seem to do a good job of defrosting meat though ... but perhaps we are doing it the wrong way?

GETTING STARTED

Here are a few notes that will help you make the most of this book.

Matrix

The matrix at the end of the book (page 171) is designed to help you maximise your use of refrigerated or pantry ingredients. It shows the entire list of recipes in the book, and then for each one it ticks off the Super Single Ingredients that feature in it. We've ticked ingredients that feature in the recipe, as well as where they feature as optional ingredients, so that if you have, say extra carrots, you can see at a glance where you could potentially use them.

Optional Extra Ingredients

We consider all of the recipes in this book to be merely the 'base case scenario'. By that we mean that to every dish you can add other, different ingredients that you may have in your kitchen. We want you to take these recipes and make them your own in new and exciting ways. So, for every recipe we have listed other ingredients that will work in that dish or to substitute for an ingredient listed in the dish. Once again, it's about maximising what you have.

Recipe Information Guide

At the top of each recipe page we have put a few pieces of information about each dish. This information is designed to let you know about the timing, portion size, freezing suitability and the use of pots and pans for each recipe. We've also included what we believe are the true qualities of each dish—such as 'Comfort Food', 'Spoil Yourself' or 'Tasty and Healthy'. All of this information is designed to help you decide what to have for dinner each night, depending on how much time you have, and of course, what food mood you are in.

WEEKLY MENUS AND SHOPPING LISTS

Just about everybody has got one of those friends who knows on 4 May what they'll be having for dinner on 12 June. For everybody else, let us say this: we know that it can sometimes be difficult to plan what you are even having for breakfast when the only thing in the cupboard is bread. In turn, coming up with seven different dinners from one weekly shop without wasting anything might seem like a tall order if you've never had a menu plan, but planning is within the realms of possibility and is a habit worth forming if you can.

We would first recommend that you flick through the recipes in this book. The recipe collection has been designed so that the same ingredients are used in many different and satisfying ways. For example, three different recipes use gnocchi, so that you use the whole packet. Or roast lamb. Roast lamb? Yes! You can cook a lovely lamb roast all for yourself and still make use of what is left over—for instance a lovely home-made lamb curry or an easy shepherd's pie.

Baby spinach leaves, coleslaw, mayonnaise and Teriyaki sauce all feature in a multitude of recipes to ensure that you get to use all of what you buy, if not this week, then next. What's more, if you don't actually feel like having to think about what you're going to eat, then we've gone one step further and created four weeks of dinner menus and the shopping lists to go with them. The aim of these weekly menus is to allow you to eat something different every night of the week, but still maximise the use of ingredients you bought in one single shop. We'd like to say up front that it's practically impossible to use absolutely everything from a weekly shop, but we feel confident that these menus will make the most of your food dollar and, for the most part, whatever is left over will keep well if stored properly.

If sticking to prescribed weekly menus isn't your thing, then don't fret. You don't have to be super-organised to make the most of what you have or to stay inspired. Just a little forethought at the supermarket and a well-stocked pantry and you are halfway there. This book is a guide to get you started and hopefully, after a while, you'll try experimenting with other ingredients and new recipes so that food and effort don't go to waste, and eating interesting meals every night of the week becomes standard.

Weekly Menu 1

Day 1 Summer Chicken Salad
(page 50)

Day 2 Mushroom Omelette (page 55)

Day 3 Creamy Bacon Pizza (page 60)

Day 4 Steak with Creamy Mustard
Sauce and Squashed Spuds (see
pages 76 and 152)

Day 5 Tuna and Bean Bake (page 85)

Day 6 Classic Fish Pouch (page 78)
and Quick Potato Salad (page 144)

Day 7 Mushroom Risotto (page 66)

Weekly Menu 1
Shopping List (for 7 dinners)

GENERAL

½ cup (100 g/3½ oz) Arborio rice

1 tin (100 g/3½ oz) mixed beans

½ sheet puff pastry

500 ml (17 fl oz/generous 2 cups) chicken or
  vegetable stock

1 tin (100 g/3½ oz) tuna in spring water

3 eggs

FRUITS AND VEGETABLES

2 lemons

5 eschalots

2 handfuls or a small bag of baby spinach or
  rocket leaves

2 cups (200 g/7 oz) medium-sized white
  mushrooms

Handful green grapes or 1 green apple

1 bunch asparagus or brocollini

1 stick celery

6 chat potatoes

BUTCHER/FISH/DELI

2 chicken tenderloins

50g (1¾ oz) bacon, diced

1 steak (of your choice)

1 salmon fillet

DAIRY/COLD SECTION

1 packet (500 g/1¼ lb) grated mixed cheese

20 g (¾ oz/¼ cup) grated (shredded)
  parmesan cheese

9–10 tbsp (135–150 ml/5–6 fl oz) sour cream

125–150 g (4–5 oz) butter

PANTRY/LONG LIFE IN FRIDGE

75 ml (5 tbsp) light olive oil

15 ml (1 tbsp) capers

45 ml (3 tbsp) mayonnaise

Mixed dried herbs

30 ml (2 tbsp) seedy or Dijon mustard

Dried tarragon

Salt and pepper

**YOU MAY HAVE THE FOLLOWING
UNCOOKED INGREDIENTS LEFT OVER FROM
THIS WEEK***

Chicken tenderloins: place them into freezer
  bags in batches of two or three and freeze

Puff pastry sheets: keeps in the freezer for
  up to 3 months

Grated (shredded) parmesan cheese:
  keeps refrigerated in an airtight container
  for a couple of weeks

Eggs: will keep for up to a month in the
  fridge

Arborio rice: keeps in the cupboard in an
  airtight container for up to 18 months

*Check out the other weekly menus and their
  shopping lists, because they may feature
  some of your leftover ingredients, too.

Weekly Menu 2

Day 1 French-style Lentils (with rice, cook a double quantity of rice to use on day 3) (page 102, 136)

Day 2 Stracciatella Soup (page 47)

Day 3 Fried Rice (page 130)

Day 4 Baked Dinner for One (page 106)

Day 5 Leftover lamb Curry (page 129)

Day 6 Mama's Lemon and Chicken Rice

(page 86)

Day 7 Quick Frittata (page 44)

Weekly Menu 2
Shopping List (for 7 dinners)

GENERAL
1 can (175 ml/6 fl oz/3/4 cup) coconut cream or milk

500 ml (17 fl oz/generous 2 cups) chicken stock

1 can (400 g/14 oz) green or brown lentils

200 g (7 oz/1 cup) short or medium grain rice

5 eggs

30 ml (2 tbsp) or 1 snack box sultanas (golden raisins)

1 small can (300 g/11 oz) diced tomatoes

- -

FRUITS AND VEGETABLES
Handful of baby spinach or rocket (optional)

2 carrots

4 eschalots

1–2 lemon

3 garlic cloves

1 pink-skinned potato

- -

BUTCHER/FISH/DELI
125g (4 oz) bacon pieces, diced

2 chicken tenderloins

2 lamb shanks or a mini lamb roast (enough for a roast plus leftovers)

- -

DAIRY/COLD SECTION
1 cup (120 g/4¼ oz) frozen mixed vegetables such as peas, carrots and corn

65 g (2½ oz) 3/4 cup grated (shredded) Parmesan cheese

15 ml (1 tbsp) sour cream (optional)

20 g (1 tbsp) marinated goat's cheese or feta in oil

45 ml (3 tbsp) butter

- -

PANTRY/LONG-LIFE IN FRIDGE
90 ml (6 tbsp) light olive oil

Curry powder

Nutmeg

Dried tarragon

15 ml (1 tbsp) soy sauce

Salt and pepper

- -

YOU MAY HAVE THE FOLLOWING UNCOOKED INGREDIENTS LEFT OVER FROM THIS WEEK*

Rice: keeps in the cupboard in an airtight container for 18 months

Sultanas (golden raisins): will keep in the cupboard for six to nine months.

Chicken tenderloins: place them into freezer bags in batches of two or three and freeze

Eggs: will keep for up to a month in fridge

Marinated goat's cheese or feta in oil: will keep refrigerated for 18 months

Frozen mixed vegetables: make sure the bag remains airtight and they will keep for 18 months in the freezer

*Check out the other weekly menus and their shopping lists, because they may feature some of your leftover ingredients, too.

Weekly Menu 3

Day 1 Spaghetti Bolognese (pages 136, 110)

Day 2 Tomato and Bacon Gnocchi
(page 63)

Day 3 Nachos for One
(using Bolognese Sauce leftovers)
(page 118)

Day 4 Salmon-baked Eggs with Tomato
Salad (pages 58, 139)

Day 5 Ham Salad (page 53)

Day 6 Shepherd's Pie with Green Salad

(pages 116, 138 also using Bolognese sauce

leftovers)

Day 7 Creamy Salmon Gnocchi (page 68)

Weekly Menu 3
Shopping List (for 7 dinners)

GENERAL

1 jar spaghetti sauce (300 ml/½ pint/1¼ cups)

1 x 400 g (14 oz) can peeled and diced tomatoes

1 packet of corn chips (individual size) (about 80 g/3 oz)

1 x 100 g (3¼ oz) can corn kernels

65 g (2½ oz/⅔ cup) pasta shapes

350 g (12 oz) gnocchi

FRUITS AND VEGETABLES

1 avocado

1 whole baby cos (romaine) lettuce

½ cup (60 g/2¼ oz) brocoli florets or chopped asparagus (small bunch)

30 cherry tomatoes (or roughly one punnet)

2 eschalots

2 garlic cloves

1 courgette (zucchini)

1 large potato

1 lemon

1 onion (small)

BUTCHER

500 g (1¼ lb) minced (ground) beef

50 g (1¾ oz) bacon

DAIRY/COLD SECTION

50 g (1 ¾ oz) butter

50 ml (2 fl oz/¼ cup) milk

3 eggs

1 tbsp marinated goat's cheese or feta in oil

120 ml (4 fl oz) sour cream

80 g (2½ oz) grated (shredded) mixed cheese

75 g (2½ oz) ham

100 g (3½ oz) smoked salmon

75 g (3 oz) grated (shredded) Parmesan cheese

PANTRY/LONG LIFE IN FRIDGE

Ground cumin

Dried mixed herbs

1 tbsp tomato ketchup

1–2 tbsp mayonnaise

Chilli powder (optional)

5½ tbsp light olive oil

Red or white vinegar

Salt and pepper

YOU MAY HAVE THE FOLLOWING INGREDIENTS LEFTOVER FROM THIS WEEK*

Bolognese sauce: freeze in individual portions for up to three months

Eggs: will keep for up to a month

Marinated goat's cheese or feta in oil: will keep refrigerated for 18 months

Gnocchi: will keep refrigerated in an airtight container for a couple of weeks or in the freezer for a couple of months

*Check out the other weekly menus and their shopping lists, because they may feature some of your leftover ingredients, too.

Weekly Menu 4

Day 1 Japanese Crumbed Chicken Salad (Quick Katsu Don) (page 92)

Day 2 Easy Stir-fry (using chicken) (page 91)

Day 3 Spaghetti and 'Meatballs' (page 81)

Day 4 Gourmet BLT (page 96)

Day 5 Spicy Red Beans (page 108)

Day 6 Salami Pizza with Green salad (using baby cos/romaine) (pages 60, 138)

Day 7 Jack of Spuds (using Spicy Red Beans leftovers, page 120)

Weekly Menu 4
Shopping List (for 7 dinners)

GENERAL
1 x 400 g (14 oz) can tomato pulp or diced and peeled tomatoes

1 Turkish bread roll or other fresh roll

25 g (1 oz/½ cup) breadcrumbs (Japanese Panko crumbs are the best and are usually available in big supermarkets)

⅔ cup (75 g/2½ oz) angel hair pasta

60 ml (2 fl oz) mayonnaise (Japanese Kewpie is recommended, again usually available in large supermarkets)

75 ml (2½ fl oz) pizza base sauce

½ sheet puff pastry

1 x 400 g (14 oz) can red kidney beans

FRUITS AND VEGETABLES
12 cherry tomatoes

3 cups coleslaw mix (without the dressing)

3 eschalots

1 baby cos

4 garlic cloves

2 handfuls baby spinach leaves

1 lemon

1 potato (pink skinned)

BUTCHER/FISH/DELI
4 bacon rashers

4 to 6 chicken tenderloins

50 g (1¾ oz) salami slices

2 sausages (pork suggested)

DAIRY/COLD SECTION
1 egg

100 g (3½ oz) grated mixed cheese

30 g (1¼ oz) grated (shredded) parmesan cheese

1 tbsp sour cream

PANTRY/LONG LIFE IN FRIDGE
Ground cumin

Chilli powder

Mixed dried herbs

100 ml (3½ fl oz) light olive oil

15 ml (1 tbsp) oyster sauce

15 ml (1 tbsp) soy sauce

75 ml (2½ fl oz) teriyaki sauce

Wasabi or horseradish cream (optional)

Salt and pepper

YOU MAY HAVE THE FOLLOWING COOKED/UNCOOKED INGREDIENTS LEFTOVER FROM THIS WEEK...

Breadcrumbs: store in an airtight container or Ziploc bag for up to 6 months

Pasta: store in an airtight container in the cupboard for up to 18 months

Pizza base sauce: stores refrigerated for up to 1 month

Chicken tenderloins or sausages: place them into freezer bags in batches of two or three and freeze

Spicy Red Beans: freeze in individual portions for up to three months.

Puff pastry sheets: keep in the freezer for up to 3 months

Grated (shredded) Parmesan cheese: keeps refrigerated in an airtight container for a couple of weeks

Eggs: will keep for up to a month

*Check out the other weekly menus and their shopping lists, because they may feature

QUICK AND LIGHT MEALS

QUICK FRITTATA

Less than 15 minutes | Vegetarian

Frittatas are Italian omelettes which are left unfolded and often finished in the oven to cook the top. The brilliant thing about them is that you can put practically anything in them and they will taste wonderful. A non-stick frying pan is highly recommended for a successful frittata. For this recipe you will need one that has an oven-proof handle.

SERVING SUGGESTION | Green Salad on page 138, Tomato Salad on page 139

INGREDIENTS

2 tbsp butter

½ cup (60 g/2 ¼ oz) frozen mixed vegetables (such as peas, carrots, corn)

Salt and pepper

3 eggs

20 g (¾ oz) marinated goat or feta cheese, crumbled

EXTRA OPTIONAL INGREDIENTS

Chopped cooked fresh vegetables such as broccoli florets, carrot, bell pepper (capsicum), courgette (zucchini), onion or mushrooms

Chopped fresh herbs such as parsley, chives, chervil.

Add some diced ham or bacon.

Add a few dollops of ratatouille (see page 104).

Use leftover roast vegetables instead of frozen ones.

PREPARATION

Preheat the oven to 180°C/350°F/Gas mark 4.

In a medium-sized frying pan set over medium-high heat, melt half of the butter until bubbling, then add the frozen vegetables, together with a pinch of salt. Heat through for 1-2 minutes, then add 2 tablespoons of cold water and cook for another 3-4 minutes or until the vegetables are just softened. You may need to add a little more water until they are sufficiently cooked. When the vegetables are soft, reduce the heat to medium. Add the remaining butter, swirling it around the pan and up the sides a little.

Crack the eggs into a bowl and whisk lightly to combine. Season generously with salt and pepper. Pour into the frying pan over the vegetables. Leave to cook for about 3 minutes, or until the base starts to solidify.

Scatter the crumbled cheese over the surface of the frittata, then place the whole pan in the oven for about 10 minutes or until the frittata is cooked through (it will no longer wobble when shaken). Use an oven mitt or kitchen towel when removing the pan from the oven as the handle will be very hot. Serve hot.

CHICKEN AND COUSCOUS SALAD

Less than 10 minutes | One-pot dish

A light but filling meal that is ready in a flash. The lemon and spice combination gives it a distinctly Middle Eastern flavour and the lettuce adds some crunch.

SERVING SUGGESTION | Needs no accompaniment

INGREDIENTS

55 g (/2 oz/⅓ cup) couscous
Salt
Pinch of ground cumin
75 ml (2½ fl oz/⅓ cup) boiling water
55 g (2 oz) cooked chicken breast (or ham or turkey), chopped
125 g (4 ¼ oz) can chickpeas (garbanzo beans) or 4-bean mix, rinsed and drained
1 eschalot, peeled and finely chopped
Handful of baby spinach, rocket (arugula) or baby cos (romaine) leaves, roughly chopped
Juice of ½ lemon
A little oil, approximately 1 tbsp

EXTRA OPTIONAL INGREDIENTS

Chopped capsicum (bell pepper), carrot or celery
Chopped hard-boiled egg
Fresh chopped parsley, chives or basil

VARIATIONS

Use a small can of tuna fish instead of the chicken breast .
For a more substantial meal, serve this salad without the meat as a side dish to a piece of grilled (broiled) chicken or fish.

PREPARATION

Put the couscous in a mixing bowl, add a few pinches of salt and a pinch of ground cumin. Pour over the boiling water, swirl around once with a spoon, and then cover completely with some plastic wrap or a well-fitting plate/lid, so that no steam can escape. Set aside for 6–7 minutes. Remove the cover and fluff through the couscous with a fork, to separate the grains a little.

To the couscous, add the chicken breast, chickpeas or beans, onions and salad leaves and stir to mix through. Add any other optional vegetables at this point, if you like.

To dress the salad, drizzle over the lemon juice and oil, taste, then add a little more ground cumin and salt, if you like.

Serve straight away or cover and refrigerate until ready to serve.

STRACCIATELLA SOUP

Less than 15 minutes | One-pot dish

A classic Italian soup. It's delicious and nourishing.

SERVING SUGGESTION | Hot buttered toast

INGREDIENTS

375 ml (13 fl oz) chicken stock

1 egg

40 g (1 ½ oz/ ½ cup) grated parmesan cheese

Pinch of nutmeg

Salt and pepper

Handful of baby spinach or rocket (arugula) (optional)

Juice of ½ lemon

EXTRA OPTIONAL INGREDIENTS

Cooked rice, for a little added bulk.

Fresh chopped herbs such as parsley or chives

Add some frozen mixed vegetables or a few gnocchi and cook them in the simmering stock.

PREPARATION

Pour the chicken stock into a medium-sized saucepan and bring to the boil.

Meanwhile, in a small bowl, beat the egg with a fork until blended, add the parmesan cheese, nutmeg and a little salt and pepper.

When the chicken stock is bubbling, add the egg and cheese mixture and gently stir with a whisk for 1–2 minutes. The egg and cheese mixture will break up, curdling into tiny strands.

Add a handful of baby spinach or rocket leaves to the pan with the lemon juice. Leave the soup to simmer for another 2 minutes.

Check for seasoning, and adjust the salt, pepper and lemon juice, if desired.

Ladle the soup into a serving bowl and enjoy it while hot.

SLIMMERS' SOUP

Less than 15 minutes | Tasty and healthy

This soup is great to have regularly if you are watching your weight, because it is so low in fat, but it's tasty too. You can add whatever veggies you like!

SERVING SUGGESTION | Crusty bread or hot toast

INGREDIENTS
375 ml (13 fl oz) chicken or vegetable stock
1 cup (250 g/9 oz) frozen vegetable mix (such as peas, carrot and corn kernels)
Handful baby spinach or rocket leaves
Salt and pepper

EXTRA OPTIONAL INGREDIENTS
Any other fresh, frozen or canned mixed vegetables.
Chopped herbs such as parsley or chives.
For extra bulk, add a couple of tablespoons of small pasta shapes or chop up a small potato and simmer it in the stock until cooked through.
Add a pinch of chilli flakes or a few drops of Tabasco sauce if you enjoy heat, or a squeeze of lemon juice, for extra flavour.

PREPARATION
In a small pan over medium-high heat, heat the stock until just simmering. Add the mixed frozen vegetables (and any pasta or potatoes, if you like) and continue to simmer until cooked through—mixed frozen vegetables will usually only require about 3–4 minutes. If using other, harder vegetables (like uncooked potato), then dice them up quite small and add a couple of minutes earlier so all of the vegetables are cooked through at the same time.

Add the spinach leaves just before serving, as they will only take 1 minute to cook.

Season with salt and pepper to taste and serve hot.

SUMMER CHICKEN SALAD

Less than 20 minutes | Spoil yourself

This salad has it all—great colour, flavour and crunch! Use sliced chicken breast instead of tenderloins if you prefer.

SERVING SUGGESTION | Serve on a bed of torn baby spinach, rocket or baby cos (romaine) leaves.

INGREDIENTS

2 chicken tenderloins
2 tbsp mayonnaise
Juice of ½ lemon
Salt and pepper
A handful of green grapes, halved and seeds removed, or half an apple, chopped
1 eschalot, peeled and finely sliced
1 stick celery, finely sliced

EXTRA OPTIONAL INGREDIENTS

Fresh chives, parsley or tarragon are lovely added to the mayonnaise dressing.

PREPARATION

Bring some salted water to a light simmer in a small pan or frying pan. Add the chicken to the water (ensure there is enough water to just cover) and poach gently for 10-12 minutes, turning once half way through the cooking time to ensure even cooking. Remove from the water with a slotted spoon and allow to cool. When cool enough to handle, slice into bite-sized pieces.

In a bowl, mix together the mayonnaise and lemon juice. Season to taste with salt and pepper.

Add the grapes, eschalot, celery and cooked chicken. Mix well to combine. Check the seasoning and adjust if required.

Serve immediately or cover and refrigerate to chill before eating.

HAM SALAD

Less than 10 minutes | Tasty and healthy

This salad is jam-packed with everyday ingredients, yet is delicious and incredibly satisfying as a meal. The tangy lemon dressing is to die-for!

SERVING SUGGESTION | Needs no accompaniment

INGREDIENTS

5–6 baby cos (romaine) leaves, washed and torn into bite-sized pieces

75 g (3 oz) shaved ham off the bone (or your favourite type of ham), cut into pieces

5 or 6 cherry tomatoes, halved

100g (3¾ oz) can corn kernels

Half an avocado, diced

Handful mixed cheese, grated

1–2 tbsp mayonnaise

Juice of ½ lemon

Salt and pepper

Light olive oil for dressing, optional

EXTRA OPTIONAL INGREDIENTS AND VARIATIONS

Chopped hard-boiled egg.

Salad vegetables .

Add some mustard to the dressing for a little zing!

Cooked diced bacon instead of ham.

Canned tuna fish instead of ham.

Baby spinach leaves instead of baby cos (romaine).

Marinated feta instead of grated cheese.

PREPARATION

Arrange the baby cos leaves on a large dinner plate. Scatter over the ham, tomatoes, corn, avocado and cheese.

To make the dressing, in a small bowl combine the mayonnaise, lemon juice and season with salt and pepper to taste. If it is too lemony or too thick, you can lengthen it a little by adding a dash of oil.

Pour the dressing over the salad ingredients and enjoy.

MUSHROOM OMELETTE

Less than 15 minutes | Vegetarian

Think omelettes are just for breakfast? Think again. This one is sensational for lunch or dinner. A non-stick frying pan is highly recommended for a successful omelette.

SERVING SUGGESTION | Green Salad on page 138, Tomato Salad on page 139

INGREDIENTS

2 tbsp butter
7 or 8 medium white mushrooms, sliced
3 eggs
Salt and pepper
Handful baby spinach or rocket (arugula) leaves
Large handful of grated (shredded) cheese

EXTRA OPTIONAL INGREDIENTS

Chopped green onion (scallion).
Chopped fresh herbs, such as parsley, chives or chervil.
Goat's cheese.
Diced ham or bacon.

PREPARATION

In a medium-sized frying pan set over a medium-high heat, melt 1 tbsp butter until bubbling then add the mushrooms. Cook until just softened, about 3–4 minutes. Remove the mushrooms from the pan using a slotted spoon and set aside.

Crack the eggs into a bowl and whisk lightly to combine. Season generously with salt and pepper.

Melt the remaining butter in a non-stick frying pan over medium heat until lightly bubbling. Pour in the egg mixture, swirling around to ensure an even layer in the pan. Allow to cook gently for 2–3 minutes, or until the base starts to set. You can shake the pan a little to gauge this.

Spread the mushrooms and baby spinach leaves (and any other optional ingredients) on half of the omelette, then cover the entire surface with grated cheese.

Cook for 2–3 minutes or until the egg is almost set – it should be firm most of the way through but resemble baked custard towards the top. Gently flip the empty side of the omelette over to cover the filled mushroom side and allow to cook for another minute in the pan.

Slide out onto a plate and enjoy while still hot.

VEGGIE COUSCOUS SALAD

Less than 10 minutes | Vegetarian

This salad is wonderful as a light meal, but can work just as well as a side dish to grilled meats, such as a chicken breast or lamb chops as well.

SERVING SUGGESTION | Needs no accompaniment

INGREDIENTS

55 g (2 oz/⅓ cup) couscous
Salt
¼ teaspoon cumin
75 ml (2½ fl oz/⅓ cup) boiling water
1/2 cup (approx. 70 g/2¾ oz) diced pumpkin or sweet potato
1 small zucchini (courgette), diced
1 tbsp butter
3 or 4 mushrooms, quartered
Pepper
20 g (¾ oz) marinated feta or goat's cheese

EXTRA OPTIONAL INGREDIENTS

Some fresh chopped herbs.
Some sliced eschalot or brown onion.
Diced red capsicum (bell pepper).

PREPARATION

In a mixing bowl, place the couscous, 3 pinches of salt and the cumin, then the boiling water. Swirl the ingredients once with a spoon, then cover completely, so that no steam can escape. Set aside for 6–7 minutes.

Cook the pumpkin and zucchini until just softened (but not mushy) either by microwaving on high in a dish of water, or simmering in some salted water for about 2 minutes.

Melt the butter in a medium-sized frying pan over medium-high heat. Once bubbling, add the cooked pumpkin, courgette and mushroom pieces. Cook for 5–6 minutes or until turning golden brown, stirring occasionally. Season well with a little salt and lots of pepper.

Remove the cover from the couscous and fluff through with a fork to separate the grains a little.

Add the hot buttered vegetables and stir through to combine. Crumble over the cheese and enjoy hot or cold.

SALMON-BAKED EGGS

Less than 30 minutes | One-pot dish | Tasty and healthy

These creamy baked eggs turn golden brown in the oven and are delicious hot or cold

SERVING SUGGESTION | Green Salad on page 138, French Beans on page 142

INGREDIENTS

A little butter, for greasing

3 eggs

1 tbsp sour cream

50 g (1¾ oz) smoked salmon, cut into thin strips

60 g (2 oz) chopped green vegetables, such as small broccoli florets or asparagus

Salt and pepper

EXTRA OPTIONAL INGREDIENTS AND VARIATIONS

Chopped fresh herbs, such as chives or dill.

Cooked frozen peas instead of fresh vegetables.

Cooked diced potato for extra bulk.

Bacon or ham and cherry tomatoes instead of salmon.

Top with some cheese, or add some chopped eschalot, for more flavour.

PREPARATION

Preheat the oven to 180°C/350°F/Gas mark 4.

Lightly grease a medium-sized ramekin or small non-stick baking dish with butter.

Crack the eggs into the ramekin or baking dish and, using a fork, just break the yolks and swirl around through the white.

Add the sour cream and stir lightly again, but don't 'beat' the ingredients together.

Add the salmon strips, vegetables and any other optional ingredients. Season well with salt and pepper and give another quick stir.

Bake in the oven for 25 minutes, or until set and turning golden on top. Enjoy straight from the baking dish.

PIZZA THREE WAYS

Less than 30 minutes | No pots or pans | Spoil yourself/Vegetarian

Mix and match toppings according to your own taste. This dish is wonderful for a relaxed weeknight dinner. Make sure you include mozzarella in the mixed cheese for the topping.

SERVING SUGGESTION | Green Salad on page 138 or Tomato Salad on page 139

INGREDIENTS

FOR CREAMY BACON PIZZA

½ sheet puff pastry or an individual pitta bread

2–3 tbsp sour cream

50 g (2 oz) bacon, diced

1 eschalot, peeled and sliced

Salt and pepper

2 handfuls mixed grated cheese

FOR SALAMI PIZZA

½ sheet puff pastry or an individual pitta bread

2–3 tbsp tomato paste (purée) or pizza-base sauce

50 g (2 oz) salami slices

2 handfuls baby spinach leaves

2 handfuls mixed grated cheese

PREPARATION

Preheat the oven to 180°C/ 350°F/ Gas mark 4.

If using puff pastry, remove a sheet from the freezer so that it starts to defrost. When it is just soft enough to cut, cut it in half and return half to the freezer for another day.

Line a large baking try with baking paper (parchment). Place the half-sheet of pastry or pita bread on the baking paper.

FOR THE CREAMY BACON PIZZA

Spread the sour cream generously over the entire pizza base, leaving 1 cm (½ in) all around the edge unfilled.

Arrange the bacon and eschalot on the cream. Season and scatter over the cheese.

Bake until golden on top and the pastry base is cooked through, about 25 minutes. Serve hot.

FOR THE SALAMI PIZZA

Spread the tomato paste generously over the entire pizza base, leaving 1 cm (½ in) all around the edge unfilled.

Arrange salami and spinach on the paste, and scatter over the cheese.

Bake until golden on top and the pastry base is cooked through, about 25 minutes. Serve hot.

Continued on page 66.

For Vegetarian Pizza

½ sheet puff pastry or an individual pitta bread

2–3 tbsp sour cream

1 large zucchini (courgette)

Handful baby spinach leaves

1 eschalot, peeled and sliced

Salt and pepper

1–2 tbsp marinated feta or goat's cheese, crumbled

Extra Optional Ingredients

Small handful chopped capsicum (bell pepper).

Mushrooms.

Halved cherry tomatoes.

Tinned pineapple.

Olives or any other topping you enjoy.

For the Vegetarian Pizza

To make a vegetarian pizza, spread the sour cream generously over the entire pizza base, leaving 1cm (½ in) all around the edge unfilled.

Arrange the zucchini, spinach leaves and the eschalot on the cream. Season and scatter over the cheese.

Bake until golden on top and the pastry base is cooked through, about 25 minutes. Serve hot.

Note: The extra optional ingredients can stay the same for all pizzas.

You can also double the recipe, as pictured, and fill the whole sheet of puff pastry make leftovers for lunch the next day).

GNOCCHI THREE WAYS

Less than 15 minutes | One pot dish

Gnocchi are small flour or potato dumplings from Italy. They are cooked, like pasta, in boiling water. There are several store-bought varieties readily available which is what we will be using here. They are usually sold in 500 g (1¼ lb) packs, which is too much for one person to consume comfortably in one sitting, so here are three different ways to use it.

SERVING SUGGESTION | Green Salad on page 138, Tomato Salad on page 139, Trio Salad on page 140, Cucumber Salad on page 141

INGREDIENTS

FOR TOMATO AND BACON GNOCCHI

175 g (6 oz) potato gnocchi (this is usually a third of a packet)
2 tsp light olive oil
50 g (1¾ oz) bacon or ham, diced
1 eschalot, peeled and sliced
10 cherry tomatoes, cut in half
Salt and pepper
Parmesan cheese, grated (shredded), to serve

FOR SPINACH AND CHICKEN GNOCCHI

175 g (6 oz) potato gnocchi (this is usually a third of a packet)
2 tsp light olive oil
50 g (1¾ oz) cooked chicken breast, chopped
1 eschalot, peeled and sliced
2 handfuls baby spinach leaves
3 tbsp sour cream
Salt and pepper
Parmesan cheese, grated (shredded), to serve

PREPARATION

Bring plenty of salted water to the boil in a heavy-based pan.

Add the gnocchi. They are ready when they float to the surface—less than 5 minutes.

Drain well and set aside.

Return the pan to the stove top, over a medium-high heat.

FOR THE TOMATO AND BACON GNOCCHI

Add the dash of oil and, once it's hot, add the bacon, eschalot, and cherry tomatoes. Cook for 4-5 minutes, or until cooked through.

Return the cooked gnocchi to the pan and stir through gently to coat with the sauce. Taste, and add salt and pepper, if required.

To finish, add the grated cheese, stir through once more and serve hot.

FOR THE SPINACH AND CHICKEN GNOCCHI

Add the dash of oil and, once it's hot, add the chicken, eschalot, spinach leaves and sour cream. Cook for 4-5 minutes, or until cooked through.

Continued on page 69.

For Creamy Salmon Gnocchi

175 g (6 oz) potato gnocchi (this is usually a third of a packet)

2 tsp light olive oil

50 g (1 ¾ oz) smoked salmon, cut in pieces

1 zucchini (courgette), ends removed and finely sliced

2 tbsp sour cream

Salt and pepper

Parmesan cheese, grated (shredded), to serve

Extra optional ingredients

Add chopped vegetables such as red capsicum (bell pepper), mushrooms, zucchini (courgettes).

Add a few fresh basil leaves or chopped chives.

Return the cooked gnocchi to the pan and stir through gently to coat with the sauce. Taste, and add salt and pepper, if required.

To finish, add the grated cheese, stir through once more and serve hot.

For the Creamy Salmon Gnocchi

Add the dash of oil and, once it's hot, add the smoked salmon, zucchini and sour cream. Cook for 4-5 minutes, or until cooked through.

Return the cooked gnocchi to the pan and stir through gently to coat with the sauce. Taste, and add salt and pepper, if required.

To finish, add the grated cheese, stir through once more and serve hot.

MUSHROOM RISOTTO

Less than 30 minutes | One-pot dish

Risotto is another hearty Italian dish that is as versatile as it is filling. It can be a meal in itself or served as a side dish to your favourite cooked meat. These recipes will make a generous meal-sized serving for one.

SERVING SUGGESTION | Needs no accompaniment

INGREDIENTS

15 ml (1 tbsp) butter
65 g (2½ oz/1 cup) sliced white medium mushrooms
1 eschalot, peeled and sliced
100 g (3¾ oz/½ cup) arborio rice
500 ml (17 fl oz/generous 2 cups) vegetable or chicken stock (salt-reduced variety)
1 tbsp sour cream
Salt and pepper
20 g (¾ oz/¼ cup) grated (shredded) parmesan cheese

EXTRA OPTIONAL INGREDIENTS

Add baby spinach or rocket (arugula) leaves
Add fresh chopped herbs such as chives, crushed garlic or sliced spring onion (scallion).
Try other cheeses.
Add bacon for extra flavour.

PREPARATION

In a small pan, or a medium frying pan, melt the butter over a medium-high heat. When the butter is golden and bubbling, add half the mushrooms and the eschalot. Cook until just softened, then add the rice.

Stir for a couple of minutes or until the grains turn semi-translucent.

Add half the stock and stir well. Stir from time to time (but not constantly) so that the rice cooks evenly and doesn't stick. Once the stock has been absorbed, add more in batches of about 100 ml (3½ fl oz/scant ½ cup), about 20–25 minutes. Don't be tempted to increase the heat—making risotto is a slow process that is worth the time and effort.

When you add the last batch of stock, add the remaining mushrooms, and the sour cream. Check the seasoning and add some salt and pepper, if required.

When the liquid is almost fully absorbed, add the cheese. Once it has melted through the dish, remove from the heat and serve hot.

CHICKEN RISOTTO

Less than 30 minutes | One-pot dish

Another variation of risotto, this time with the added depth of chicken pieces and the freshness of green vegetables.

SERVING SUGGESTION | Needs no accompaniment

INGREDIENTS

1 tbsp butter

2 chicken tenderloins, diced

100 g (3¾ oz/½ cup) arborio rice

500 ml (17 fl oz/generous 2 cups) vegetable or chicken stock (salt-reduced variety)

120 g (4¼ oz/1 cup) mixed green vegetables (a mix of small broccoli florets and frozen peas works well)

1 tbsp sour cream

Salt and pepper

20 g (¾ oz/¼ cup) grated (shredded) parmesan cheese

EXTRA OPTIONAL INGREDIENTS

Add baby spinach or rocket (arugula) leaves.

Add some fresh chopped herbs, such as chives, some crushed garlic.

Add sliced spring onion (scallion) or eschalot.

Try other cheeses.

PREPARATION

In a small saucepan or a medium frying pan, melt the butter over a medium-high heat. When the butter is golden and bubbling, add the chicken. Cook until just coloured, then add the rice. Stir for a couple of minutes or until the grains turn semi-translucent.

Add half of the stock and stir well. Stir from time to time (but not constantly) so that it cooks evenly and doesn't stick. Once the stock has been absorbed, add more in batches of about 100 ml (3 ½ fl oz/scant ½ cup), about 20-25 minutes. Don't be tempted to increase the heat—making risotto is a slow process that is worth the time and effort.

When you add the last 100 ml (3 ½ fl oz/scant ½ cup) of stock, add the vegetables and the sour cream.

When the liquid is almost fully absorbed, add the cheese. Once the cheese has melted through the dish, remove from the heat and serve hot.

PASTA SALAD

Less than 15 minutes | Spoil yourself!

This pasta salad is easy to make and is bursting with the flavor of cherry tomatoes. Use leftover cooked pasta if you have some, instead of cooking it from scratch.

SERVING SUGGESTION | Needs no accompaniment

INGREDIENTS

500 ml (17 fl oz/generous 2 cups) water
salt
65 g (2½ oz/⅔ cup) pasta shapes
140 g (4½ oz) can corn kernels
5 or 6 cherry tomatoes, sliced in half
1 eschalot, peeled and finely sliced
50 g (1¾ oz) soft goat's cheese or marinated feta cheese, crumbled
1 tbsp mayonnaise
Pepper
Light olive oil

EXTRA OPTIONAL INGREDIENTS

Use a squeeze of lemon juice or a small dash of vinegar instead of mayonnaise.
Add fresh chopped herbs, especially basil, for flavour.

PREPARATION

Bring the salted water to the boil in a saucepan.

Add the pasta and swirl it around a couple of times in the first few minutes to ensure that it doesn't stick together.

While the pasta is cooking, prepare the other ingredients.

Once the pasta is cooked (usually 8-12 minutes for pasta shapes—check the manufacturer's cooking guide), drain off the water and then combine all of the ingredients in a small mixing bowl.

Check the seasoning and adjust if required.

Tip: For a fuller meal, poach a couple of chicken tenderloins and cut into pieces before adding to the dish.

PASTA CARBONARA

Less than 15 minutes | Spoil yourself!

The Italians used to make a version of this dish for the British and American troops during the war, knowing how much they loved bacon and eggs. It is a classic dish, popular all over the world for its rich and satisfying flavor, but it is quick and easy to make.

SERVING SUGGESTION | Green Salad on page 138, Tomato Salad on page 139, Trio Salad on page 140, Cucumber Salad on page 141

INGREDIENTS

500 ml (17 fl oz/generous 2 cups) water
Salt
75 g (3 oz/⅔ cup) pasta (any shapes)
1 egg
55 g (2 oz/½ cup) frozen peas
Light olive oil
75 g (3 oz) bacon, chopped
1 tbsp grated (shredded) parmesan cheese
Pepper

EXTRA OPTIONAL INGREDIENTS

Add chopped vegetables such as red capsicum (bell pepper), mushrooms, zucchini (courgettes) or a handful of baby spinach leaves.
Add a few fresh basil leaves.

Tip: The egg makes a sauce for this pasta dish, but if you prefer you could add a spoonful of sour cream or pizza-base sauce.

PREPARATION

Bring the salted water to the boil in a saucepan. Add the pasta and swirl it around a couple of times in the first few minutes to ensure that it doesn't stick together. Depending on what pasta size you are using this will take 8-12 minutes simmering time (check the manufacturer's cooking guide).

Crack the egg into a bowl and whisk lightly with a fork. Set aside.

Tip the peas into the water with the pasta for the last few minutes of cooking so that they are just soft. Drain the pasta and peas through a colander. Set aside.

Return the empty saucepan to a medium heat, add a little oil and the chopped bacon. Cook until golden. Add any other vegetables you like at this stage and cook for a couple of minutes.

Return the peas and pasta to the pan. Pour in the beaten egg and quickly stir the egg, bacon, pasta and peas together. Add the cheese and stir again.

Remove from the heat, tip into a large bowl and add a little twist of pepper.

GARLICKY CHICKEN PASTA

Less than 30 minutes | One-pot dish

This dish is brimming with the bold flavor of garlic and the delightfully slippery texture of saucy pasta. Enjoy.

SERVING SUGGESTION | Needs no accompaniment

INGREDIENTS

500 ml (17 fl oz/generous 2 cups) water

Salt

65 g (2½ oz/⅔ cup) pasta shapes (or 2 bird's nests of angel hair)

2 tbsp light olive oil

2 or 3 chicken tenderloins, diced

2 or 3 cloves garlic, peeled and crushed (minced)

125 ml (4 fl oz/½ cup) chicken stock

½ tbsp butter

⅓ bunch chives, chopped

Pepper

Parmesan cheese, for topping

EXTRA OPTIONAL INGREDIENTS

Baby spinach or rocket (arugula) leaves.

Add cream.

Add cooked broccoli florets or zucchini (courgette) slices to add more green.

PREPARATION

Bring the salted water to the boil in a saucepan. Add the pasta and swirl it around a couple of times in the first few minutes to ensure that it doesn't stick together. Cook following the manufacturer's instructions. Drain and keep the pasta warm.

Return the pan to a medium-high heat and add the oil. Once hot, fry the chicken pieces on all sides until browned—about 4–5 minutes on each side. Add the garlic and stir quickly for about 1 minute, or until it has softened, but not browned.

Add the stock and reduce the heat to medium. Cook for about 10 minutes or until the sauce has reduced.

To thicken the sauce, add the butter and stir through, then add the chives. Taste and add salt and pepper, if required. Cook for another 1–2 minutes.

Pour the hot pasta into the pan and stir through to coat with the sauce. Serve hot, topped with Parmesan cheese.

SUBSTANTIAL MEALS

THREE IDEAS FOR A STEAK DINNER

Less than 15 minutes | Spoil yourself!

You may not eat steak every night of the week, so when you do, it should be special. Here are three quick and easy ways to turn it into something truly delicious.

SERVING SUGGESTION | Mashed Potato on page 145, Squashed Spuds on page 152

INGREDIENTS

½ bunch of asparagus or broccolini
½ lemon
1 steak of your choice
Salt and pepper
Light olive oil

FOR MUSHROOM SAUCE

Small knob of butter
3–4 mushrooms, sliced
1 tbsp sour cream

FOR CREAMY MUSTARD SAUCE

Small knob of butter
1 tbsp seedy or Dijon mustard
1 tbsp sour cream

FOR RED WINE SAUCE

1 tbsp butter
2 eschalots, peeled and finely chopped
120 ml (4 fl oz/½ cup) red wine

EXTRA OPTIONAL INGREDIENTS

Any fresh herbs, chopped.
Crushed (minced) garlic would work well in any of these sauces.

PREPARATION

Steam or blanch the asparagus in the microwave or in a pan of lightly simmering water, for about 3 minutes or until just softening. Set aside and keep warm. Season the steak on both sides and brush with a little oil (see Cooking Steaks page 134). For medium-rare, fry in a non-stick frying pan over medium-high heat until juices start to emerge from the top. Turn the steak over and fry for another 2–3 minutes. Turn out onto a serving plate and keep warm.

FOR THE MUSHROOM SAUCE

In the same frying pan over medium heat, melt the butter. Add the mushrooms and cook for a few minutes or until lightly golden and softened. Add the sour cream and stir through evenly. Cook for another minute.

FOR THE CREAMY MUSTARD SAUCE

In the same frying pan over medium heat, melt the butter and add the mustard and sour cream. Stir through evenly. Allow to cook for 2 minutes until thickened.

FOR THE RED WINE SAUCE

In the same frying pan set over medium heat, melt the butter and add the eschalots. Cook for a few minutes until softened. Add the red wine and cook until the liquid is reduced and thickened, about 2–3 minutes.

Taste and season the sauce. Pour it over the steak. Squeeze lemon juice over the vegetables and serve.

CLASSIC FISH POUCH

Less than 25 minutes | No pots or pans

Pouches are an easy, no-fuss way to prepare fish dishes. Using regular store-bought aluminium foil, they are simple to make and you can add practically any of your favourite ingredients. The fish stays lovely, tender and moist.

SERVING SUGGESTIONS | French Beans on page 142, Mashed Potato on page 145, Quick Potato Salad on page 144, Squashed Spuds on page 152

INGREDIENTS
4 or 5 asparagus spears, halved and wooden ends discarded
1 salmon steak or fillet
Salt and pepper
½ tsp dried tarragon
1 tbsp capers
½ lemon
1 tbsp butter

EXTRA OPTIONAL INGREDIENTS AND VARIATION
Add a few baby spinach leaves or broccolini to the pouch, if you like.
Add a couple of sprigs of fresh dill.
Use a white fish fillet, such as barramundi, if you prefer.

PREPARATION
Preheat the oven to 180°C/350°F/Gas mark 4.

Tear off a large piece of aluminium foil then place a smaller piece of baking paper on top of it. Place the asparagus pieces on the paper in the middle in a flat pile.

Season the salmon steak with salt and pepper then place on top of the asparagus. Sprinkle over the tarragon, toss a few capers over the salmon and squeeze over the juice from your half lemon. Top with the butter.

Fold up the foil into a parcel so that no air can escape. Place on a baking tray and cook for 15–20 minutes (it may puff up with steam). Unfold the foil carefully, allowing the steam to escape. Serve hot.

ASIAN FISH POUCH

Less than 25 minutes | No pots or pans | Tasty and healthy

Tender fish with that classic Asian combination of flavours—soy, ginger and garlic.

SERVING SUGGESTION | Lemon Vegetables page 151, rice page 136

INGREDIENTS

2 or 3 pieces broccolini, halved

1 clove garlic, crushed (minced)

1 white fish fillet, such as ling or barramundi (approximately 150–200 g/5–7 oz)

1 tbsp soy or hoisin sauce

1 tsp fresh ginger, grated (shredded)

EXTRA OPTIONAL INGREDIENTS

Add a few baby spinach leaves, asparagus pieces or very thinly sliced carrot or red capsicum (bell pepper) to the pouch.

PREPARATION

Preheat the oven to 180°C/350°F/Gas mark 4.

Tear off a large piece of aluminium foil and place the purple sprouting brocolini pieces in the middle in a flat pile. Scatter the garlic over the top. Add any optional vegetables to the pouch here.

Put the fish fillet on top of the vegetables, then pour the soy or hoisin sauce over the fish (making sure that it doesn't seep over the edge of the foil). Scatter over the ginger. Fold up the foil into a parcel so that no air can escape. Place on a baking tray and cook for 15–20 minutes (it may puff up with the steam that forms). When cooked, unfold the foil carefully, allowing the steam to escape. Serve hot.

QUICK SPAGHETTI AND 'MEATBALLS'

Less than 20 minutes | Comfort food | All-in-one meal

Want to enjoy meatballs without having to make them? This recipe cleverly uses the seasoned mince from sausages as 'meatballs', so it is quick to prepare but packed full of authentic Italian flavors, including garlic and tomato.

SERVING SUGGESTION | Needs no accompaniment

INGREDIENTS

500 ml (17 fl oz/generous 2 cups) water

Salt

75 g (3 oz/⅔ cup) angel hair pasta if in short pieces, or a handful if not

½ tbsp light olive oil

2 pork sausages

2 cloves garlic, crushed (minced)

5 or 6 cherry tomatoes, halved

1 tsp mixed dried herbs

1–2 tbsp pizza-base sauce or tomato paste (purée)

Salt and pepper

Generous sprinkling of grated (shredded) parmesan cheese

EXTRA OPTIONAL INGREDIENTS

Sliced mushrooms or spinach leaves wilted into the sauce.

Diced bacon for extra flavour.

A pinch of chilli powder for extra kick.

PREPARATION

In a medium pan set over high heat bring the salted water to the boil. Add the angel hair pasta and cook for 3–4 minutes, or until cooked (following the manufacturer's instructions). Remove from the heat, drain and set aside while you prepare the sauce.

Meanwhile split the skin coating the sausages and squeeze out small balls of the sausage meat, about the size of a ping pong ball.

In the same pan (for convenience), heat a little oil over medium-high heat. Cook the meatballs in the oil until browned on all sides, about 5 minutes.

Add the garlic and tomatoes. Then add the herbs and the pizza sauce or tomato paste.

Taste and add salt and pepper if needed, and a little water if the sauce is too thick. Cook for 2–3 minutes.

Return the cooked pasta to the pan and stir in. Add the cheese and stir through again. Serve hot.

SALMON TERIYAKI WITH MASH

Less than 25 minutes | All-in-one meal | Spoil yourself!

Teriyaki sauce is a great way to add flavour to meats, with its savory caramel and ginger undertones. And it complements vegetables well too!

SERVING SUGGESTION | Needs no accompaniment

INGREDIENTS

1 salmon fillet or steak
50 ml (2 fl oz/¼ cup) teriyaki marinade
1 tbsp light olive oil
115 g (4 oz/1 cup) frozen peas
2–3 tbsp milk or cream or stock
Knob of butter
Salt and pepper

EXTRA OPTIONAL INGREDIENTS AND VARIATION

Use some homemade vegetable mash here instead of making the pea mash from scratch—see page 145
Add 1 tsp wasabi (Japanese horseradish) to the mash for some extra kick and authenticity.
Use chicken tenderloins or strips of beef instead of salmon, if you prefer.
Add some sliced vegetables to the pan when cooking the meat—red and green capsicum (bell pepper) work well.

PREPARATION

Slice the salmon fillet into smaller strips and place in a medium mixing bowl. Pour over the teriyaki sauce and set aside for at least 15 minutes. Stir the salmon from time to time to ensure that it marinates evenly.

While the salmon is marinating, you can make your green pea mash. Either simmer the peas in 500 ml (17 fl oz) salted water for 5 minutes or place them in 500 ml (17 fl oz) of salted water in a microwave-proof bowl and cook on high for about 4 minutes.

When cooked, drain off the water and add 2 tbsp of liquid (milk, cream or stock) and a small knob of butter (approximately 1 tsp). Add the wasabi if you are using it.

Using your hand-held blender or liquidizer, puree the peas until they are soft, adding a little more liquid if required. The consistency of the mash is entirely up to you. If you want to achieve a very smooth puree, then keep blending and adding small amounts of liquid and butter until you get the result you want. A chunky mash will take half the time and taste great, too.

In a non-stick frying pan set over low-medium heat, add a little oil and then add the marinated salmon strips. Cook slowly, turning the salmon gently until cooked through, 3–4 minutes. Teriyaki sauce contains sugar, which will burn if the pan is too hot.

Pour the remaining marinade over the salmon for the last minute or so, so that it bubbles in the pan and thickens slightly.

To serve, spoon a layer of vegetable mash onto a plate, place the salmon on top and pour the sauce over both.

TUNA AND BEAN BAKE

Less than 30 minutes | All-in-one meal

This recipe is great to make from store cupboard ingredients at the end of the week when the fridge is practically bare.

SERVING SUGGESTION | Needs no accompaniment

INGREDIENTS

85 g (3¼ oz) can tuna in spring water
115 g (4 oz) can mixed beans or plain white beans, such as cannellini
2–3 tbsp sour cream
1 eschalot, peeled and sliced
1 tsp mixed dried herbs
Salt and pepper
A little butter, for greasing
Small handful mixed grated (shredded) cheese

EXTRA OPTIONAL INGREDIENTS

Add some fresh vegetables, such as broccoli florets or chopped celery, or frozen ones such as peas.

PREPARATION

Preheat the oven to 180°C/350°F/Gas mark 4.

In a small mixing bowl, combine the drained tuna, beans, sour cream, eschalot and herbs.

Season with a little salt and pepper.

Grease a 10 cm (4 in) diameter ramekin with butter and spoon in the tuna mixture. Top with the grated cheese.

Bake for 20-30 minutes or until golden brown on top.

Serve hot, straight from the dish.

MAMA'S LEMON AND CHICKEN RICE

Less than 20 minutes | Comfort food

A nourishing meal that we used to love as children. This dish is lemony and tastes so creamy, though it contains no cream. What's not to love about that?

SERVING SUGGESTION | French Beans on page 142, Lemon Vegetables on page 151

INGREDIENTS

500 ml (17 fl oz/ generous 2 cups) water

Salt and pepper

65 g (2½ oz/⅓ cup) rice

2 chicken tenderloins, chopped into bite-sized pieces

1 egg

2–3 tbsp lemon juice

20 g (¾ oz/¼ cup) parmesan cheese, grated (shredded)

1 tbsp butter

EXTRA OPTIONAL INGREDIENTS

Add 55 g (2 oz/½ cup) cooked peas, 60 g (2¼ oz/½ cup) cooked asparagus or zucchini (courgette) pieces, or a couple of handfuls of baby spinach or rocket (arugula) leaves at the end.

PREPARATION

Pour cold salted water into a medium pan and set over a high heat. Add the rice and bring to the boil.

Once boiling, turn down the heat and simmer gently for about 4 minutes. Add the chicken and leave to simmer again for another 5–6 minutes, or until both are cooked through. (Taste a few grains to check.) Drain through a colander and set aside.

Meanwhile, in a small bowl, gently whisk together the egg, lemon juice and cheese.

Return the saucepan to the hotplate, this time over a low heat and melt the butter. When it is bubbling, add the hot drained rice and chicken, and add the egg mixture and stir through well to combine. Add any other cooked vegetables you may be using. Season well with salt and pepper.

Serve hot.

QUICK LAMB CASSEROLE

Less than 25 minutes | Comfort food

This is a hearty French-style casserole which will have you licking your plate. The chives add freshness at the end of the cooking.

SERVING SUGGESTION | Needs no accompaniment

INGREDIENTS

1 tbsp oil

125–150 g (4 ¼–5 oz) lamb, diced (rump or leg—this is usually available already diced at your supermarket or butcher)

1 eschalot, peeled and sliced

125 g (4¼ oz) can of mixed beans, drained of their liquid

120 ml (4 fl oz/½ cup) chicken stock or white wine

120 ml (4 fl oz/½ cup) cream or sour cream

⅓ bunch fresh chives, chopped

Salt and pepper

EXTRA OPTIONAL INGREDIENTS AND VARIATION

Add some sliced garlic.

Add some mixed frozen vegetables, or add some baby spinach leaves to the last few minutes of cooking.

Use diced potato or carrot instead of beans.

PREPARATION

Heat the oil in a medium pan over medium-high heat until hot. Add the lamb and brown on all sides for 2–3 minutes.

Add the eschalot to the pan and cook for another 1–2 minutes.

Add the beans and the chicken stock or wine, cover and cook for 8–10 minutes.

Remove the lid and cook for another 7–8 minutes or until the liquid has reduced. The dish should simmer lightly, otherwise the beans will be too mushy.

Add the cream and half the chives and cook for 2–3 minutes or until thickened.

Just before serving, add the remaining chives and stir through, for a fresh oniony kick.

GET YOUR GREENS STIR-FRY

Less than 10 minutes | Tasty and healthy

This recipe is terrific as it uses up any green vegetables you may have, and makes its sauce from long-life fridge and pantry items. It's so easy to double the quantity for leftover lunch the next day!

SERVING SUGGESTION | Rice on page 136

INGREDIENTS

2 tbsp light olive oil

125–150 g (4½–5 oz) beef, chicken or pork, cut into thin strips

2 handfuls baby spinach leaves

60 g (2¼ oz/½ cup) small broccoli florets

60 g (2¼ oz/½ cup) other sliced green vegetables, such as snow peas (mangetout), celery, beans, zucchini (courgettes)

1 tsp ginger (fresh or from a jar), grated (shredded)

1 tbsp soy sauce

A little water

EXTRA OPTIONAL INGREDIENTS

Add some fresh chopped chilies if you like a little heat. The amount will depend on the strength of your chilies, so start with a small amount, such as half a teaspoon. A tablespoon of fresh chopped coriander (cilantro) would work well.

PREPARATION

In a frying pan set over a high heat, pour 15 ml (1 tbsp) of the oil and heat until very hot.

Add the meat and fry for 1–2 minutes or until just browned.

Remove the meat with a slotted spoon and set aside. Add the remaining oil to the pan, heat, then add the remaining vegetables and the ginger. Stir until softened.

Return the meat to the pan and add the soy sauce. Add 1–2 tablespoons of water to extend the sauce, if desired.

Stir to combine and heat through. Serve hot.

EASY STIR-FRY

Less than 10 minutes | Tasty and healthy

This dish is served over a bed of rice, but if you don't have time to cook that too, have it without!

SERVING SUGGESTION | Rice on page 136

INGREDIENTS

2 tbsp light olive oil
125–150 g (4¼–5 oz) beef, chicken or pork, cut into thin strips
2–3 handfuls ready-made coleslaw mix (no dressing)
1 clove garlic, crushed (minced)
1 tbsp oyster sauce
1 tbsp soy sauce

EXTRA OPTIONAL INGREDIENTS

Chopped vegetables such as broccoli, zucchini (courgette), celery, beans, snow peas (mangetout).
If you have some ground (minced) ginger or chilli, add a pinch.

PREPARATION

In a frying pan set over high heat, heat 1 tablespoon of the oil until it is very hot.

Add the strips of meat and cook for 1–2 minutes or until just browned.

Remove the meat using a slotted spoon and set aside. Add the remaining oil to the pan with the other vegetables and garlic. Stir until softened.

Return the meat to the pan and add the oyster and soy sauces.

Stir to combine and heat through well.

Serve hot.

JAPANESE CRUMBED CHICKEN SALAD (QUICK KATSU DON)

Less than 20 minutes | Comfort food

Spoil yourself with this deliciously crunchy meal consisting of crumbed chicken and tangy coleslaw on the side.

SERVING SUGGESTION | Needs no accompaniment

INGREDIENTS

2 or 3 chicken tenderloins

75 ml (2½ fl oz/⅓ cup) teriyaki sauce or marinade (optional)

25 g (1 oz/½ cup) breadcrumbs (Panko crumbs work best)

1 egg

5–6 tbsp light olive oil

1–2 tbsp mayonnaise (Japanese Kewpie mayonnaise tastes the best)

Wasabi or horseradish cream (optional)

65 g/2½ oz/1 cup) ready-made coleslaw mix

EXTRA OPTIONAL INGREDIENTS

For the salad: finely grated ginger, finely sliced celery, or some corn kernels.

Add some lemon juice to the dressing, if you like.

PREPARATION

In a small bowl, marinate the chicken in the teriyaki sauce for 10–15 minutes (this step is optional—you can crumb your tenderloins without marinating first).

Beat the egg in another small bowl using a fork.

Tip the breadcrumbs onto a plate.

Dip each tenderloin in the egg, then roll it in the breadcrumbs to coat it evenly.

Heat the oil in a small frying pan over medium-high heat. When hot, add the chicken and cook until golden brown on one side, about 3–4 minutes, then turn and cook the other side for another 3–4 minutes or until golden brown. Reduce the heat to low and leave to cook for another 3–4 minutes, to ensure it is cooked through. You may need to turn them again once or twice to ensure even cooking.

Meanwhile, prepare the salad. Mix the mayonnaise and the wasabi or horseradish together in a small bowl. Add the coleslaw mix and stir through.

Serve the tenderloins hot with the crunchy salad on the side.

SOLO STROGANOFF

Less than 20 minutes | Comfort food

The trick with this dish (or any dish using beef strips) is not to overcook the meat. Don't be tempted to wait until the meat is fully browned before adding the next ingredients.

SERVING SUGGESTION | Serve over a bed of rice (page 136) to soak up the sauce or steam some chat potatoes . Tastes wonderful with French Beans on page 142

INGREDIENTS
1–2 tbsp light olive oil or butter
65 g (2½ oz/1 cup) mushrooms, cleaned and sliced
1 eschalot, peeled and sliced
125–150 g (4½–5 oz) beef, cut into strips
1 tbsp paprika
Chilli powder, to taste (optional)
Salt and pepper
1 tbsp sour cream

EXTRA OPTIONAL INGREDIENTS
A squeeze of lemon juice will freshen the flavours at the end of cooking.
Fresh herbs such as chives or parsley complement this dish particularly well.
Throw in some spinach leaves for some extra greens.

PREPARATION
In a medium fry-pan over medium-high heat, heat 1 tbsp of the oil or butter then add the mushrooms and cook until softened and golden, about 4 minutes. Add the eschalot and cook for a couple of minutes, until just softening.

Remove both from the pan to a small plate and return the pan to the heat. If need be, add a little more oil. When hot again, add the beef strips and season well with the paprika, chilli powder (if using), salt and pepper.

Once the meat is just browning and the paprika is becoming fragrant, add the sour cream and stir well to coat the meat. Return the mushroom and eschalot to the pan and combine all the ingredients. Cook for another couple of minutes or until heated through.

Serve hot.

GOURMET BLT

Less than 15 minutes | Comfort food

If you're going to have a sandwich for dinner, then this is the one to have. Toasted Turkish bread is delightfully crusty and soft at the same time and works so well with the bacon, tangy dressing and salad.

SERVING SUGGESTION | Needs no accompaniment

INGREDIENTS

2 rashers (strips) bacon
7–8 cherry tomatoes, quartered
1 eschalot, peeled and finely diced
Salt and pepper
1–2 tbsp mayonnaise (Kewpie tastes the best)
Juice of ½ lemon
Pinch chilli powder (optional)
1 Turkish bread roll, sliced in half, or bread for one person
A few leaves of baby cos (romaine) lettuce, washed and finely shredded

EXTRA OPTIONAL INGREDIENTS

Add some torn fresh basil leaves to the tomato salsa.
Add a layer of avocado if you have some spare.

PREPARATION

Place a medium pan over medium-high heat. Add the bacon and cook to your liking. Drain on kitchen paper to remove any excess oil.

Meanwhile, mix together the tomatoes and eschalot in a small mixing bowl and season well with salt and pepper.

Combine the mayonnaise, lemon juice and chilli powder in a small bowl or cup.

Toast or grill the Turkish bread slices and place on a serving plate. On one slice (the top), add a generous dollop of mayonnaise dressing.

On the other slice (the bottom) layer the bacon rashers, then the tomato and eschalot mixture. Pile on a layer of shredded lettuce, then cap with the mayonnaise bun.

Enjoy hot.

Tip: You shouldn't need to use oil or butter to cook bacon as it will 'leach' fat of its own in the cooking process.

MAKING AND USING LEFTOVERS

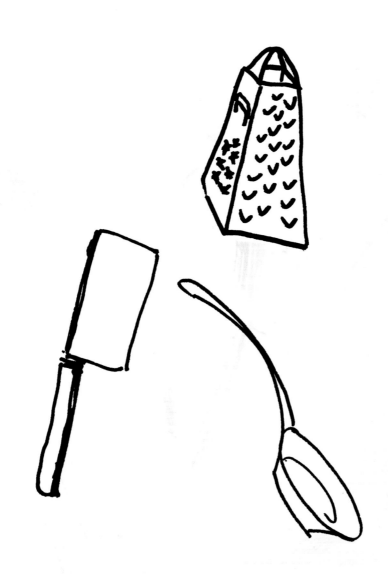

POTATO AND LEEK SOUP

30 minutes | One-pot dish | Freezes well
Makes a double portion

An old favourite that never fails to warm your heart, and it's so easy to make.

SERVING SUGGESTION | A few fresh chopped herbs such as chives or parsley . Crusty bread or hot buttered toast

INGREDIENTS

1 leek
1 tbsp butter
2 medium potatoes, peeled and diced
500 ml (17 fl oz/generous 2 cups) chicken stock
Salt and pepper

EXTRA OPTIONAL INGREDIENTS

A little sour cream or a square of processed cheese for extra depth of flavour.
Add some cooked bacon pieces towards the end of the cooking time.

PREPARATION

Trim the ends off the leek and remove and discard the outer two or three layers. Slice the leek in half lengthways and rinse well under a running tap. Slice each half thinly, to produce half-moons.

Melt the butter in a small pan over medium heat and add the leek. Allow to fry until soft and transparent, but do not allow to brown.

Add the potato cubes to the pan and then add the chicken stock. Turn the heat up to medium-high and cover. Allow the soup to gently simmer for 15–20 minutes or until the potato is soft.

Remove the pan from the heat and blend the contents with a hand-held blender. The soup will be quite thick, so you can add a little cream or extra stock if you want to thin it a little.

Taste and season with salt and pepper if needed. Serve hot, ladled into a soup bowl.

FRENCH-STYLE LENTILS

less than 15 minutes | One-pot dish | Freezes well
Makes a double portion

Lentils are earthy and nourishing, and the French know how to set them against relishing flavours like tarragon and eschalot to really get them going. This dish has a certain 'je ne sais quoi'!

SERVING SUGGESTION | Mashed Potato on page 145, serve with rice (see page 136)

INGREDIENTS

1 tbsp light olive oil
1 eschalot, peeled and finely diced
75 g (3 oz) bacon, chopped (optional)
1 carrot, peeled and finely diced
1 x 400 g (14 oz) can brown or green lentils, drained
125 ml (4 fl oz/½ cup) chicken stock
1 tsp dried tarragon
1 tbsp sour cream (optional)
Salt and pepper

EXTRA OPTIONAL INGREDIENTS

1 stick of celery, ends removed and finely sliced, baby spinach leaves.
Add a chopped potato or some pumpkin for more bulk.

PREPARATION

In a frying pan set over medium heat, lightly fry the eschalot in a little oil until softened but not brown. Add the bacon pieces, if using, and cook for 3–4 minutes.

Add the carrot and other optional vegetables, if using, and cook for another 2–3 minutes, or until just softened.

Pour the lentils into the pan, stir gently, then add the chicken stock and the tarragon. (If you stir the lentils too vigorously they will become mushy.) Reduce the heat and leave to simmer gently until most of the liquid has evaporated.

Add the sour cream. Taste for seasoning and add more salt and pepper, if desired.

Serve hot or cold.

Tip: Freshen with a squeeze of lemon juice just before serving.

RATATOUILLE

35 minutes | Creates Ratatouille leftovers | Freezes well
Makes 4 portions

A hearty and versatile vegetable stew, brimming with flavour and colour. Include a few dollops in a frittata.

SERVING SUGGESTION | Works as a side dish with grilled (broiled) lamb chops, chicken breast or a steak.

INGREDIENTS

75 ml (2½ fl oz/⅓ cup) light olive oil
1 medium onion, peeled and chopped
1 clove garlic, peeled and crushed (minced)
1 small eggplant (aubergine), chopped into bite-sized pieces
1 medium zucchini (courgette), chopped (if small cut into rounds, if large cut into half moons)
2 medium tomatoes, peeled and chopped
1 red capsicum (bell pepper), thinly sliced
2 sprigs fresh thyme
1 tsp dried oregano
140 g (4¾ oz) tub tomato paste purée
5 tbsp water, red wine or chicken stock
Salt and pepper

OTHER RECIPES THAT USE THIS SAUCE:

Shepherd's Pie on page 116
Savoury Scroll on page 125
Lamb Chops with Ratatouille on page 113
Quick Beef Goulash on page 122
Provençale Chicken on page 123
Minestrone on page 124
Pasta Primavera on page 126

PREPARATION

First of all, to remove any bitterness from the eggplant, the pieces must be salted. To do this, place them in a colander and sprinkle liberally with salt. Leave to sit for about 10 minutes. You will notice a clear liquid emerging from the eggplant, and this contains the bitterness of the vegetable. Rinse all the pieces well under a running tap to remove the salt and bitter liquid. Pat dry with kitchen paper or a clean tea towel.

In a large pan set over medium heat, heat about 1 tbsp olive oil and then add the onion and garlic. Cook until translucent, about 3 minutes. Remove from the pan with a slotted spoon and set aside.

Add some more oil to the pan and cook the eggplant in batches until just brown (the eggplant will absorb a lot of oil, so you will need to keep adding oil).

Return all of the eggplant to the pan then all of the other ingredients, starting with the vegetables and finishing off with the tomato paste and liquid. Stir well to combine.

Taste and season if needed (remember that you've already salted the eggplant).

Reduce the heat to low, cover and allow to cook through for 20–35 minutes, stirring occasionally.

If your ratatouille is too liquid, remove the lid and allow to reduce.

BAKED DINNER FOR ONE

90 minutes | Creates lamb leftovers | Spoil yourself!

Feel like an easy, scrummy baked dinner? Try this one for one!

SERVING SUGGESTION | French Beans on page 142 or Lemon Vegetables on page 151

INGREDIENTS

1–2 lamb shanks depending on their size (or more if you wish to create leftovers) or
1 chicken leg (Maryland)
A little light olive oil
Salt and pepper
Oven roasting bag
1 potato (with pink skin, such as Desiree or Pontiac)
1 carrot
1 eschalot

EXTRA OPTIONAL INGREDIENTS

Any other vegetables that you enjoy roasted–such as tomatoes or sweet potato, some dried mixed herbs for roasting your lamb.

Other recipes which use this dish:
Individual Shepherd's Pie on page 116
Leftover Lamb Curry on page 129

PREPARATION

Preheat the oven to 190°C/375°F/Gas mark 5.

Rub the lamb shanks or chicken leg all over with a little oil and season well with salt and pepper (and any dried herbs you may like to use).

Place in an oven roasting bag on a medium baking tray, and bake for 50-60 minutes (Maryland) and 75-90 minutes (shank).

Meanwhile, prepare the vegetables. Prick the potato skin a few times with a fork then place it in a microwave-proof bowl with a little water and cover and cook in the microwave until just softening (about 5-8 minutes). Then place it in the oven to become crisp for the last 20 minutes of cooking.

Slice off the two ends of the carrot and eschalot, then peel and rub with a little oil. Put both whole into the dish with your baking meat for the last 20 minutes of cooking.

Remove the meat from the oven and leave to rest for 5 minutes before removing from the oven bag, to rest.

Serve hot with the roasted vegetables and any other side dishes.

SPICY RED BEANS

less than 15 minutes | Freezes well | Makes Spicy Red Bean leftovers
Makes 4 portions

This dish is teaming with the flavours of tex-mex spices. A delicious meal when served with rice, it also works well in nachos or on a jacket potato.

SERVING SUGGESTION | A little sour cream and grated cheese on top,
or serve on a bed of rice–see page 136

INGREDIENTS

1–2 tbsp light olive oil
2 eschalots, peeled and roughly chopped
75 g (3 oz) bacon, diced (optional)
1 garlic clove, peeled and roughly chopped
400 g (14 oz) can red kidney beans, drained
400 g (14 oz) can tomato pulp or passata
1 tbsp ground cumin
Chilli powder (to taste)
Mixed dried herbs
Salt and pepper

EXTRA OPTIONAL INGREDIENTS

Browned minced (ground) beef, sliced
mushrooms, sliced red capsicum
(bell peppers)

Other recipes which use this sauce:
Nachos for One on page 118
Jack of Spuds on page 120

PREPARATION

In a large frying pan heat 1 tablespoon of oil over medium-high heat, then add the eschalots. Cook until just softened. Add the bacon pieces, and, after about 2-3 minutes, or when they are almost cooked, add the garlic and cook for another 30 seconds, but don't let the garlic turn brown.

Add the kidney beans and the tomato pulp.

Season with the cumin, chilli, dried mixed herbs, and salt and pepper. Reduce the heat to medium. The bean mixture should be left to cook for a few minutes or until the sauce is reduced and thickened. Check the seasoning and adjust to suit your tastes, if necessary.

Serve hot.

BOLOGNESE SAUCE

30 minutes | Freezes well | Creates Bolognese leftovers
Makes 4 portions

An old favourite, but don't feel like you always have to use this sauce with pasta. Try some of the recipes in the following pages that also use this sauce, such as a jacket potato.

SERVING SUGGESTION | Serve with Pasta, see page 136, and a little grated (shredded) parmesan cheese

INGREDIENTS
1–2 tbsp light olive oil
1 small onion, peeled and finely chopped
1 clove garlic, peeled and crushed (minced)
500 g (1¼ lb) minced (ground) beef
400 g (14 oz) can diced peeled tomatoes
1 tbsp tomato ketchup
1 small jar of favourite store-bought spaghetti sauce (approx. 300 g/11 oz)
½ tbsp mixed dried herbs
Salt and pepper

EXTRA OPTIONAL INGREDIENTS
Finely chopped celery, eggplant (aubergine), zucchini (courgette), or carrot.
Freshly chopped herbs.

Other recipes that use this sauce:
Shepherd's Pie on page 116
Nachos on page 118
Savoury Scroll on page 125
Jack of Spuds on page 120

PREPARATION
In a large pan over medium heat, add 1 tbsp of oil. When hot, add the onion and cook until almost transparent. Add the garlic. Cook for 1 minute and then remove the onion and the garlic using a slotted spoon.

Divide the mince into two equal portions and cook in batches in the pan used to cook the onions. Add and heat a little more oil, if required.

Stir continuously, pressing the mince down and chopping through any large lumps of meat with your wooden spoon. Once browned, remove the mince from the pan and drain any liquid into a separate bowl then continue with the next batch.

Once cooked, return all of the mince, onion and garlic to the pan.

Add tomatoes, the ketchup, spaghetti sauce and dried herbs, then season with salt and pepper. Stir to combine.

Turn down the heat to low and cook for 20 minutes—checking and stirring every 5 minutes.

Taste the sauce and adjust the seasoning. If it is too liquid, allow to simmer for a few minutes to reduce.

Divide into portions and freeze when cold or serve immediately.

FRAGRANT LAMB CHOPS WITH RATATOUILLE

Less than 20 minutes | Uses Ratatouille leftovers

This one is too easy. Just cook your favourite lamb chops and serve with piping hot Ratatouille on the side. The flavours complement each other well.

SERVING SUGGESTION | Mashed Potato on page 145, Squashed Spuds on page 152

INGREDIENTS

2 tbsp light olive oil

1 sprig of fresh thyme and 1 sprig of fresh rosemary or 1 teaspoon dried mixed herbs

1 clove of garlic, crushed (minced)

Salt and pepper

2–3 lamb cutlets or your favourite lamb chops, enough for 1 person (approx 200 g/7 oz)

Ratatouille portion (see page 104)

EXTRA OPTIONAL INGREDIENTS

You could add other herbs or a squeeze of lemon juice to the marinade.

PREPARATION

Place the oil, herbs, garlic and a little salt and pepper in a mixing bowl and stir through. Add the lamb cutlets and coat with the oil. Set aside to marinate for at least 10 minutes, or if longer, place in the refrigerator to marinate.

Re-heat the portion of ratatouille.

Meanwhile, bring a frying pan to a medium-high heat. Cook the cutlets for 3–4 minutes on each side, or to your liking, turning once.

Serve hot, with the Ratatouille on the side.

LEFTOVER VEGETABLE SOUP

40 minutes | Makes use of spare vegetables | Freezes well
Makes 4–6 portions

Any leftover vegetables are suitable for this soup. It can be different every time you make it. The ingredients here are just a suggestion.

SERVING SUGGESTION | Crusty bread roll or hot buttered toast

INGREDIENTS

1–2 tbsp butter or oil
1 potato, peeled and diced
1 small leek, ends and outer leaves removed, washed and finely sliced
1 carrot, peeled and chopped
1–2 sticks of celery, ends removed, finely sliced
1 small onion, peeled and chopped
1 litre (1¾ pints/4 cups) chicken stock
2 tbsp chopped parsley
Salt and pepper
Use sour cream instead of plain cream, if you have it

EXTRA OPTIONAL INGREDIENTS

Any other vegetables (fresh, frozen or canned).
Cream or sour cream.
Some lemon juice.
Herbs for added flavour.
Some cooked diced bacon.

PREPARATION

In a large pan over medium heat melt the butter and add all of the chopped vegetables.

Stir well to coat and allow the vegetables to cook gently in the butter for 3–4 minutes or until the onion and leek are softened.

Pour in the chicken stock and raise the heat to medium-high so that the soup simmers. Allow to simmer for 20–25 minutes or until all of the vegetables are cooked and soft.

Remove from the heat and, using a handheld blender, carefully blend the soup until you reach a smooth, even consistency.

Serve topped with a little cream or sour cream and some chopped parsley.

INDIVIDUAL SHEPHERD'S PIE

Less than 25 minutes | Uses Bolognese/Ratatouille/Roast Lamb leftovers | Freezes well

A small and easy version of this iconic dish. Great for using all sorts of leftovers.

SERVING SUGGESTION | Green Salad on page 138, French Beans on page 142

INGREDIENTS

Either 1 portion of Bolognese sauce OR 125–150 g (4¼–5 oz) leftover cooked diced roast lamb OR 1 portion of Ratatouille for a vegetarian version

1 large potato

1 tbsp butter

A little milk

Salt and pepper

Grated (shredded) parmesan cheese

EXTRA OPTIONAL INGREDIENTS

If using meat as your base, add a handful of frozen peas or baby spinach, a small tin of corn kernels drained of liquid, or some chopped green beans to your pie.

PREPARATION

Preheat the oven to 180°C/350°C/Gas mark 4.

Lightly grease the base and sides of a small ovenproof dish such as a ramekin or pie dish (about 10 cm/4 in diameter). Tip the base sauce (Bolognese, diced lamb, or ratatouille) into the dish.

Peel and chop the potato into small cubes the size of dice (this will speed up the cooking process). Cook by either bringing to the boil in 500 ml (17 fl oz/2 cups) salted water for about 10 minutes (or until soft) or placing in a microwave-proof bowl in 500 ml (17 fl oz/2 cups) salted water for about 5 minutes (or until soft).

In a mixing bowl, combine the cooked potato and butter by mashing with a fork or vegetable masher (you can also use your hand-held blender). You want your mash to be quite thick and not runny, but you can add a little milk if it is looking too dry and lumpy. Season well with salt and pepper.

Top the pie base with potato, smoothing it over the entire surface. Cover with the grated (shredded) cheese and bake for 20 minutes, or until the cheese is golden brown.

NACHOS FOR ONE

Less than 15 minutes | Uses Bolognese/Spicy Red Beans leftovers | Comfort food

Nachos is such a popular café dish, but there's no reason not to enjoy this easy version at home!

SERVING SUGGESTION | Needs no accompaniment

INGREDIENTS

1 portion of Bolognese Sauce
1 tbsp cumin
Chilli powder, to taste
Or
1 portion of Spicy Red Beans
80–100 g (3–4 oz) corn chips
Couple of handfuls grated mixed cheese
3 or 4 cherry tomatoes sliced in half
½ avocado, diced
1 tbsp sour cream

EXTRA OPTIONAL INGREDIENTS

Any other salad vegetables you like, such as corn kernels, diced cucumber or carrot.

PREPARATION

Preheat the grill (broiler) to medium-high or the oven to 180°C/350°F/Gas mark 4.

Heat the Bolognese Sauce, in a small saucepan over medium heat, if using. Add the cumin and chilli powder and leave to cook through for 3–4 minutes.

If using red beans, simply re-heat your portion.

Meanwhile, scatter the corn chips over a heat-resistant plate, then cover with the grated cheese. Place under the grill or in the oven until the cheese melts.

Remove carefully as the plate will be hot.

Arrange the beef or beans mix in the middle of the corn chips. Scatter over the tomatoes and avocado and top with a dollop of sour cream. Enjoy hot.

JACK OF SPUDS

Less than 20 minutes | Uses Bolognese Sauce/Spicy Red Beans leftovers | All-in-one meal

We used to love this dish on Friday nights from our local take-away shop. Make it at home and enjoy the richness of Bolognese combined with the crunchy tang of coleslaw—it's quite divine.

SERVING SUGGESTION | Needs no accompaniment

INGREDIENTS
1 large pink-skinned potato (such as Desiree or Pontiac)
1 portion of Bolognese Sauce mixture OR
1 portion of Spicy Red Beans
2–3 tbsp coleslaw (see page 149)
1 tbsp sour cream
Handful grated cheese

EXTRA OPTIONAL INGREDIENTS
Grated carrot, lettuce leaves, sautéed mushrooms

PREPARATION
Preheat the oven to 180°C/350°F/Gas mark 4.

Make a cross in the potato skin using a sharp knife. Put the potato in a microwave-proof bowl with a couple of tablespoons of water. Cover and cook until cooked through, about 5–6 minutes, depending on the microwave and the size of your potato.

Place in a hot oven for 5–10 minutes, or until the skin is crispy.

Meanwhile, reheat the Bolognese Sauce or Spicy Red Beans.

Remove the potato from the oven and put on a serving plate. Split open using the cross made previously. Fluff up the potato using a fork and top with Bolognese Sauce or Spicy Red Beans. Serve with coleslaw, and top with sour cream and cheese.

Eat straight away.

QUICK BEEF GOULASH

Less than 25 minutes | Uses Ratatouille leftovers

Goulash is a meat and vegetable stew from Eastern Europe. While there are many different versions, they all use paprika, which combines here with sour cream to make this dish both smooth and slightly piquant.

SERVING SUGGESTION | Squashed Spuds on page 152, or add some cooked diced potatoes to the last 10 minutes of cooking, for an all-in-one meal.

INGREDIENTS

A little light olive oil

125–150 g (4¼–5 oz) diced beef or beef stir-fry strips

1 tbsp paprika (sweet or hot, depending on your taste)

¼ tsp chilli powder, or to taste (optional)

1 portion of Ratatouille, see page 104

125 ml (4 fl oz/½ cup) beef stock

1 tbsp sour cream

Salt and pepper

EXTRA OPTIONAL INGREDIENTS

A squeeze of lemon juice just before serving will freshen the flavour.

You could throw in a handful of gnocchi and an extra ½ cup of beef stock when adding the ratatouille for a complete meal.

PREPARATION

In a deep frying pan set over medium-high heat, heat a little oil and then brown the beef strips.

Sprinkle over the paprika and chilli powder and season with salt and pepper.

Add the Ratatouille and the beef stock and stir through. Turn down the heat to medium and allow to reduce for about 15 minutes, or until the sauce is thick.

Just before serving, add the sour cream and stir through. Check the seasoning and adjust if necessary. Serve hot.

PROVENÇALE CHICKEN

Less than 25 minutes | Uses Ratatouille leftovers | Freezes well

You'll be surprised how a hint of vinegar and capers will change the flavours of the Ratatouille.

SERVING SUGGESTION | Serve with Rice on page 136 or Pasta on page 136 or French Beans on page 142

INGREDIENTS

A little light olive oil
2–3 chicken tenderloins
1 portion of Ratatouille
1 tsp red wine vinegar
50 ml (1¾ fl oz) chicken stock or water
1 tsp capers
Salt and pepper

EXTRA OPTIONAL INGREDIENTS

Fresh chopped basil or parsley.

PREPARATION

In a non-stick frying pan set over medium heat, cook the chicken pieces in a small amount of oil until golden on all sides, about 3 minutes on each side.

Add the Ratatouille and the red wine vinegar and stir to combine. Lower the heat and allow to simmer gently for 15 minutes. If the mixture starts to get a little dry, add some chicken stock or a little water.

In the last few minutes of cooking, add the capers and stir again. Add any fresh herbs here, if you are using. Season with salt and pepper. Serve hot.

MINESTRONE SOUP

Less than 20 minutes | Uses Ratatouille leftovers | One-pot dish

This hearty and healthy vegetable soup makes use of Ratatouille leftovers. Minestrone is a classic Italian soup made by cooking vegetables and pasta together in stock.

SERVING SUGGESTION | Crusty bread roll and butter. A dollop of sour cream or grated cheese in the middle, to serve

INGREDIENTS

1 portion of Ratatouille
1 small can (85 g/3½ oz) mixed beans, drained
25 g (1 oz/¼ cup) small pasta shells or macaroni
375 ml (13 fl oz) chicken or vegetable stock (salt reduced if possible)
Salt and pepper

EXTRA OPTIONAL INGREDIENTS

Any other vegetables, such as carrot, potato, beans, peas, etc., chopped.
Fresh chopped herbs, such as parsley, basil or chives, or a couple of frozen herb cubes, thrown in, if you have them.

PREPARATION

In a medium pan, gently heat the leftover ratatouille. Add the beans and the dry pasta and stir through once or twice.

Add the stock and allow to simmer for 10–15 minutes, or until the vegetables and pasta are just cooked. Season with salt and pepper. Serve hot.

SAVOURY SCROLLS

30 minutes | Uses Bolognese Sauce or Ratatouille leftovers

Don't be put off by the use of pastry. It will be in the oven within 5 minutes, then you can sit back and relax.

SERVING SUGGESTION | Green Salad on page 138, Tomato Salad on page 139, Trio Salad on page 140, Cucumber Salad on page 141

INGREDIENTS
½ sheet puff pastry
Handful baby spinach leaves
1 portion of Bolognese Sauce OR 1 portion of Ratatouille
Handful grated (shredded) cheese

EXTRA OPTIONAL INGREDIENTS
A few sliced mushrooms.

PREPARATION
Preheat the oven to 180°C/350°F/Gas mark 4.

Remove a sheet of puff pastry from the freezer and, when just soft enough, cut in half and return half to the freezer for another day.

Line a flat baking tray (sheet) with baking paper and put the half-sheet of pastry on top.

Spread the spinach leaves over the pastry. Top with the Bolognese Sauce or Ratatouille, followed by the grated cheese (and any other optional ingredients).

Using the short side, roll up the pastry to form a scroll. Tidy any ingredients that have slipped out when rolling. Make a criss-cross pattern on top of the scroll with a sharp knife. This allows the pastry to give a little in the oven and creates a nice pattern on top.

Bake for about 25 minutes, or until golden brown. Serve hot.

PASTA PRIMAVERA

Less than 20 minutes | Uses Ratatouille leftovers | One-pot dish

This dish uses Ratatouille as the base to your pasta sauce. Delicious, and fresh as the springtime.

SERVING SUGGESTION | Green Salad on page 138

INGREDIENTS

500 ml (17 fl oz/generous 2 cups) water

Salt

75 g (3 oz/⅔ cup) pasta (penne or another shape of your choosing)

1 tbsp light olive oil

approx. 60 g (2¼ oz/½ cup) fresh or frozen chopped vegetables (e.g. peas, carrot, corn, asparagus pieces, broad beans, small florets of broccoli)

1 portion of Ratatouille

Sprinkling of grated (shredded) parmesan cheese

Pepper

OPTIONAL EXTRA INGREDIENTS

Fresh chopped herbs, such as parsley, basil or chives, or a couple of frozen herb cubes, if you have them.

Diced, cooked bacon for extra flavour.

Baby spinach or rocket leaves for some extra greens.

PREPARATION

In a medium pan, bring the salted water to the boil and cook the pasta according to the packet instructions.

Drain off the water and set side.

Return the pan to a medium-high heat and add the oil. Add the vegetables and allow to cook for 2–3 minutes, or until just softened.

Add the Ratatouille and stir through. Once hot, add the cooked pasta and stir through to coat with the sauce. Add the grated cheese and stir through.

Taste and add salt and freshly cracked pepper, if desired. Serve hot.

LEFTOVER LAMB CURRY

30 minutes | Uses lamb leftovers | Comfort food

This mild curry is a great way to use leftover cooked lamb from a roast.

SERVING SUGGESTION | Rice on page 136 or Couscous on page 137

INGREDIENTS

1–2 tbsp light olive oil

125–150 g (4¼–5 oz) leftover cooked lamb, diced (or use fresh chicken, lamb or beef, if you prefer)

1 eschalot, peeled and sliced

1 clove garlic, crushed (minced)

1 tbsp curry powder

1 small can (300 g/5 oz) diced tomatoes, or about 10 cherry tomatoes, halved

1 small can (175 ml/6 fl oz¾ cup) coconut milk

40 g (2 tbsp) or snack-sized box of sultanas (golden raisins)

Salt

EXTRA OPTIONAL INGREDIENTS

Add ½ cup of fresh, frozen or canned vegetables to the last few minutes of cooking.

Add some diced potato for a fuller meal that won't need a rice accompaniment.

Add some fresh chopped herbs, such as coriander (cilantro) or basil.

Add some chilli powder.

Use some stock for the cooking sauce.

PREPARATION

Heat the oil in a medium saucepan over medium-high heat. Add the diced lamb and heat through for 2 minutes (or brown well if using fresh meat, 3–4 minutes).

Remove the meat from the pan and set aside. Add a little more oil to the pan.

Add the eschalot and garlic. Stir continuously and cook until just softening, about 2 minutes. Do not allow to burn. Add the curry powder and cook for 1–2 minutes, or until the spices are fragrant.

Return the meat to the pan, then add the tomatoes, the coconut milk and the sultanas.

Reduce the heat to medium and cook for about 20 minutes, uncovered, so that the sauce thickens.

Serve hot, on a bed of rice, if desired.

FRIED RICE

Less than 15 minutes | Uses leftover Rice

For nights when you've got some leftover cooked rice. It's a meal in itself!

SERVING SUGGESTION | Serve as a meal on its own or as a side dish with your favourite meat.

INGREDIENTS

60 g (2¼ oz/½ cup) mixed frozen vegetables (such as peas, carrot, corn)
1–2 tbsp light olive oil
50 g (1¾ oz) bacon, diced
1 eschalot, peeled and roughly chopped
1–2 garlic cloves, crushed (minced)
1 tbsp soy sauce
65 g (2½ oz/⅔ cup) leftover cooked rice

OPTIONAL EXTRA INGREDIENTS

Fresh diced vegetables such as broccoli florets, red capsicum (bell pepper), beans, carrot, celery or spring onion (scallions)
Add an egg, lightly beaten, for extra protein

PREPARATION

Microwave on high or simmer the frozen vegetables in water until just softened, about 2 minutes.

In a frying pan set over high, heat the oil and add the bacon pieces. Cook for 1-2 minutes, or until sizzling, then add the eschalot and garlic. Cook for 1 minute but don't let it burn.

Add the cooked mixed vegetables and the soy sauce. Stir through. Add the rice. (Add the egg, if using and stir in really well until cooked through.)

Continue to cook for another 3-4 minutes, or until the rice is heated through.

Check for seasoning. If it needs a dash more soy sauce, or some pepper, then add it. Serve hot.

EASY MEATS AND SIDE DISHES

QUICK MEAT, POULTRY AND FISH

(THAT YOU CAN MIX AND MATCH WITH OUR SIDE DISHES)

You know, you don't always have to have a particular 'dish' for dinner. Sometimes you just feel like meat with something on the side. But what is the best way to cook meats to make them a little more interesting? Here are our recommendations for some popular meats. Try mixing them with some of the easy side dishes from the back of the book.

Cooking and Enjoying Steak

For such a popular cut of meat, it's amazing how many questions we get on cooking steak successfully at our workshops. There are a few simple rules to follow which will have you enjoying your favourite steak at home, and not just at the Steak House.

Firstly, brush the meat with oil and season your steak before you put it in the pan. Don't put oil, butter or fat in the pan itself.

Secondly, the cooking times for steak vary according to a couple of things—the thickness of the steak is one, and how you like your steak cooked is the second crucial variable. Here is a rough cooking guide for a 2cm (¾ in) thick piece of steak over medium-high heat:
- 2–3 minutes on each side for rare.
- 4 minutes on each side for medium.
- 5–6 on minutes on each side for well-done.

Take care to turn the meat only once (this goes for all meats, not just steak) as otherwise you will keep re-cooking the same outside parts and the meat will dry out. If you think the outside is getting too charred but it is still rare on the inside, lower the heat for the second side or pop the steak into a hot oven (180°C/350°F/Gas mark 4) for a few minutes to finish cooking through.

One way to see if your steak is cooked to your liking is to press down on the centre of it. The steak will feel soft when still rare; slightly firmer and spongy when medium; and firm when wel done. Good chefs will suggest that you leave your steak to rest for 2–3 minutes before eating, as it helps the juices settle. If you do this, cover it with foil to keep it warm during the process.

When serving, place a generous knob of butter on the top and let it melt all over the steak. Finish with a squeeze of lemon juice. Most good steak sauces are usually mostly butter anyway, so why fuss?

Another tip: if you've cooked a delicious steak or sausages one night, then once the pan has cooled down, refrigerate as is (with all the yummy meat juices and fat). The following night, use the same pan to make a delicious Steak-pan Omelette. The flavours of the meat will take your omelette to a whole new level.

Chicken Breasts

Use a non-stick pan for chicken. If you have quite a large portion of chicken breast, slice it in half lengthways, to form a butterfly: it will cook more evenly this way. Use a mixture of half oil and half butter in a medium-hot pan. Season generously with salt and pepper half-way through cooking. Once the first side is golden (after about 6-7 minutes), turn it over and cook the second half for about the same length of time. If you are not sure, use a knife to check if it's cooked through to the centre. The meat should be white and the juices clear. When almost cooked, pour a little cream, stock or white wine into the pan (1-2 tablespoons), add some dried tarragon, and cook for another 2 minutes. Pour the sauce over the chicken when serving.

Pork Chops

Season chops with salt and white pepper. Heat a mixture of oil and butter in a medium-hot pan. Turn once, when the chops have turned a deep golden colour on the first side, about 4-5 minutes. Cook on the second side for another 4-5 minutes or until just cooked through. Remove the pork and set aside, then add a little Dijon mustard and cream to the pan, or pour in a shot of sweet vermouth if you have any. Pour this sauce over the pork when serving. Also check out the dessert section. Our Caramelised Apple recipe works a treat with pork chops.

Lamb Chops

Season chops with oil, salt, pepper and a good sprinkling of mixed dried herbs. Add some chilli flakes if you like a little heat. Place them in a hot pan and cook to your liking. Turn only once. When serving, squeeze over a little lemon juice.

Sausages

Pierce a couple of holes in each sausage. If you are cooking a couple, use a small pan. Rub the pan with a very small amount of oil or use a spray oil. Use a medium heat to ensure even cooking and remember that sausages take longer to cook than you might think—about 15-18 minutes to be cooked through—so don't be tempted to use a high heat, otherwise they will be burnt on the outside and raw on the inside (think: mate's BBQ). Add a couple of whole peeled eschalots to the pan while cooking for a great onion accompaniment.

Fish Fillets

Use a non-stick pan for fish. Lightly oil and season the fish with salt but don't add any oil to the pan. Use a medium-high heat for fish and turn only once. Cook skin-side down first if it has skin. Sprinkle over some herbs, such as dill, tarragon or chives, for the last 2 minutes of cooking, or throw in some capers. Serve with a small knob of butter on top.

QUICK AND EASY CARBS

As with vegetable side dishes, cooking the traditional 'carb' accompaniments like rice and pasta to go with meat dishes can seem disheartening for one person. We've included recipes that make cooking them easier, and, most importantly, faster, too.

Pasta

Use pasta shapes such as penne, spirals, macaroni or bowties, rather than spaghetti because they are easier to cook in a small pan, and easier to measure for portion control.

Store your pasta shapes in a large airtight container with the right measuring scoop or cup kept permanently inside it. After a while, by using your regular measuring cup and the right level of water in the pan, cooking pasta for one will become an absolute dream.

Easy Cooking Method

Fill a kettle with water and boil.

Place a small saucepan over high heat and add 500 ml (17 fl oz/generous 2 cups) hot water from the kettle. Add a pinch of salt. Add the pasta and wait for the water to come to the boil again. Cook until al dente (check the packet instructions). Remove from the heat, then drain through a colander.

For one person use:
- 65 g (½ oz ⅔ cup) pasta shapes
- 500 ml (17 fl oz/generous 2 cups) water

Rice

Rice can be boiled much like pasta, though not all rice types will lend themselves to this method of cooking, but short and medium grain rice will, so do give it a try.

As with pasta, if you can store your rice in an airtight container with the right measuring scoop or cup permanently living inside it, the job will seem that much easier each time.

Easy Cooking Method

Place a small saucepan over high heat and add 500 ml (17 fl oz/generous 2 cups) cold water. Add a pinch of salt to the water, then 70 g (2¾ oz/⅓ cup) rice and bring to the boil. Then simmer until the rice is cooked through (usually about 7 or 8 minutes of simmering). Drain off the water using a fine colander or a sieve.

Couscous

Couscous is much faster and easier to prepare than rice or pasta and is just as filling and delicious when served with the right main meal. Use it as an accompaniment to curries or stews. It just soaks up sauce and is great in salads, too, dressed with a oil and lemon juice.

Easy Cooking Method:

Place 55 g (2 oz/⅓ cup) couscous into a small, heat-resistant mixing bowl. Add a pinch of salt, then pour over 75 ml (2 ½ fl oz/⅓ cup) boiling water (from the kettle) and swirl the bowl around so that the level of couscous is even in the bowl.

Cover tightly with cling film (plastic wrap) or aluminium foil so that no air can escape (the couscous cooks using the trapped steam). Set aside for 5–6 minutes then remove the covering. Fluff up the grains using a fork to separate them.

GREEN SALAD

Less than 15 minutes

If you're put off having a side salad because you don't have time to make a dressing, this dish is for you.

INGREDIENTS
Salad leaves for 1 person (baby spinach, baby cos (romaine) lettuce, rocket (arugula), or your preferred leaf)
½ lemon
Some light olive oil
Salt and pepper

EXTRA OPTIONAL INGREDIENTS
Some chopped avocado or cucumber, a finely chopped eschalot.
Fresh chopped herbs, such as parsley, chives or basil.

PREPARATION
Wash and dry the salad leaves and, if need be, tear or chop into bite-size pieces.

Put the leaves in a small bowl, then squeeze over the juice from the half lemon. Add a little oil and mix through. Taste, and if required add more of both, and some salt and pepper to taste.

TOMATO SALAD

Less than 15 minutes

This is great as a side dish, or try it served on top of some crusty bread for a great home-made bruschetta.

INGREDIENTS
10 cherry tomatoes, halved
1 small eschalot, peeled and sliced
1 tbsp marinated goat's cheese or feta
Some light olive oil and a splash of red or white wine vinegar
Salt and pepper

EXTRA OPTIONAL INGREDIENTS
Fresh chopped herbs such as parsley, chives or basil.

PREPARATION
In a small bowl, mix together the tomatoes and eschalot and then crumble through some marinated cheese.

Add a little oil, vinegar and salt and pepper, to taste.

TRIO SALAD

Less than 15 minutes

The variety of colours and flavours in this salad makes it a great accompaniment to grilled meats. You can scatter it over nachos, too!

INGREDIENTS

5–6 cherry tomatoes, halved
1 small Lebanese cucumber, sliced
1 small can (85 g /3 ½ oz) corn kernels, drained
A little red or white wine vinegar
A little light olive oil
Salt and pepper

EXTRA OPTIONAL INGREDIENTS

Fresh chopped herbs such as parsley, chives or basil, a chopped eschalot.

PREPARATION

In a small bowl, mix together the three vegetables and then add a dash of your favourite vinegar (no more than 1 tsp). Then drizzle over a little oil and stir through.

Add a little salt and pepper and check for seasoning. Adjust if required.

CUCUMBER SALAD

Less than 15 minutes

A creamy, crunchy side dish that goes well with spiced dishes or grilled meats.

INGREDIENTS
1 tbsp sour cream
1 small Lebanese cucumber, finely sliced
Chopped chives
Salt and pepper

EXTRA OPTIONAL INGREDIENTS
Other fresh chopped herbs such as parsley or basil.

PREPARATION
Mix the sour cream in a bowl so it is soft and runny, then add the slices of cucumber, the chives and a little salt and pepper.

Check for seasoning. Adjust if required. Serve cold.

FRENCH BEANS

Less than 15 minutes

Beans work so well with the oniony flavor of eschalot. This side is the perfect addition to practically any meat.

INGREDIENTS
Generous handful French (green) beans, ends removed
Salt
1 small eschalot, peeled and chopped or 1 garlic clove, crushed (minced)
Knob of butter or dash of light olive oil

EXTRA OPTIONAL INGREDIENTS
Chilli flakes, chopped parsley, toasted almonds, squeeze of lemon juice.

PREPARATION
If you like, you can remove the ends from the beans and rinse well.

Bring a small amount of salted water to a simmer in a small saucepan. Add the beans and simmer for 3–4 minutes or until just softening (you can cook for longer if you prefer). Drain, then rinse the beans under a cold running tap.

Melt the butter in a small saucepan over medium-high heat and add the eschalot or garlic, and cook until just softened, but do not allow to brown.

Add the beans and toss together.

Season with salt to taste.

EASY MIXED VEGETABLES

Less than 15 minutes

A different use of your coleslaw mix, this time cooked with a more-ish lemon butter sauce.

INGREDIENTS

Couple of handfuls of ready-made coleslaw mix
Juice of ½ lemon
A knob of butter
Salt and pepper

PREPARATION

Place the coleslaw mix in a small pan set over medium-high heat, and add a couple of tablespoons of water. Cover and cook for 3–4 minutes or until the cabbage and carrot are just softening. Add the lemon juice and butter, and season to taste with salt and pepper. Serve hot.

QUICK POTATO SALAD

Less than 15 minutes

INGREDIENTS

2–3 chat (new) potatoes, rinsed and quartered
1 tbsp mayonnaise
1 tsp seedy or Dijon mustard
1 eschalot, peeled and sliced
Salt and pepper

EXTRA OPTIONAL INGREDIENTS

Any fresh herbs, chopped.
Corn kernels, sliced celery.
Hard-boiled egg.
Cooked bacon pieces .
A few halved cherry tomatoes.
Add some sour cream to the dressing.

PREPARATION

Cook the potato pieces by either microwaving on high in salted water for 4 minutes, or simmering in a pan of salted water for about 6 minutes, or until the pieces are soft but not disintegrating.

In a small mixing bowl, combine the mayonnaise, mustard, eschalot and a little salt and pepper.

Add the cooked potatoes to this mixture and stir through to coat with the dressing. Serve warm or cold.

MASHED POTATO

Less than 15 minutes

An easy version of a classic side dish. You don't have to use only potatoes, add some carrot, pumpkin or sweet potato, too!

INGREDIENTS

160 g (5¼ oz/1 cup) peeled and diced potato/
carrot/pumpkin/kumera pieces or a
combination
1 tsp butter
1 tbsp milk
Salt and pepper

PREPARATION

Firstly, cook the vegetables by either simmering in a pan of salted water for 7-8 minutes or until quite soft, or place in the microwave in plenty of salted water and cook on high for 6 minutes.

Once soft, strain off the water and in a bowl, and mash the vegetable pieces, butter and milk together by using a fork, masher or stick blender.

Tip: This makes one quantity of mash, but you can easily double or triple the amount and freeze leftover portions to use another day, but the cooking time of the vegetables will need to increase for larger amounts.

SAUTÉED MUSHROOMS

Less than 15 minutes

This recipe is a fabulous side dish for meats, but if you want a simple meal then just have it on toast. It's nutritious, too.

INGREDIENTS
1–2 tbsp butter
A couple of handfuls of sliced mushrooms
Pinch of mixed dried herbs
Juice of ½ lemon
Salt and pepper

EXTRA OPTIONAL INGREDIENTS
Add 1 tbsp cream or sour cream in the final stages of cooking for a creamy side dish.
Add some fresh herbs such as parsley, chives or thyme for extra flavour.

PREPARATION
In a non-stick frying pan set over medium-high heat, melt the butter until bubbling. Add the sliced mushrooms and herbs and cook for about 10 minutes, or until softened and any liquid has evaporated.

Add the lemon juice. Season with salt and pepper. Stir to combine. Serve hot.

CLASSIC COLESLAW

Less than 15 minutes

A tangy, crunchy salad that works well with sausages, steak and chicken.

INGREDIENTS
Couple of handfuls of ready-made coleslaw mix
1 tbsp mayonnaise
Juice of ½ lemon
Salt and pepper

EXTRA OPTIONAL INGREDIENTS
Add a small can of corn kernels, drained,
for extra bulk.
Chopped celery and spring onion (scallions) or
eschalot can also be added.
Add a snack-box of sultanas (golden raisins) for
sweet contrast.
Add a little sour cream to add a creamy flavour.
Add a pinch of cayenne pepper
for a hint of spice.

PREPARATION
Combine all of the ingredients in a bowl and serve.

If you have time to refrigerate the mixture for a little while, the flavours will develop. The longer, the better.

LEMON VEGETABLES

Less than 15 minutes

It's amazing how a squeeze of lemon can transform veggies into a real dish.

INGREDIENTS

Selection of mixed green vegetables, for one (such as asparagus spears, zucchini (courgette), snow peas (mangetout), broccoli, spinach leaves, celery stalks, sliced fennel), sliced into batons

Juice of ½ lemon

Dash of light olive oil

Salt

EXTRA OPTIONAL INGREDIENTS

Chop up some fresh herbs and add them; chives and parsley would work well.

PREPARATION

Cook the vegetables either by simmering in some water for 3–4 minutes or steaming until cooked through (but not mushy) or using the microwave.

Drain off any water and drizzle the lemon juice and oil over the veggies.

Season lightly with salt and enjoy.

SQUASHED SPUDS

Less than 15 minutes

A different way to bake potatoes that leaves their skin crunchy and their insides fluffy.

INGREDIENTS

2–3 chat (new) potatoes
A little light olive oil
Salt—coarse sea salt if you have it

EXTRA OPTIONAL INGREDIENTS

Whole fennel or cracked pepper, sprinkled over the top. You could also put some grated cheese on top for the last 10 minutes of baking.

PREPARATION

Preheat the oven to 190°C/375°F/Gas mark 5.

Cook the whole chat potatoes until just cooked through, either using a microwave, or simmering them in a small pan of water.

Line a flat baking tray with a sheet of baking paper. Put the cooked potatoes on top and, using a potato masher, squash each potato until it splits open and is at least half-way flattened.

Brush the squashed potatoes with a little oil (or spray them with some oil from a can) and sprinkle over some coarse sea salt.

Bake for about 20 minutes, or until crispy and just turning golden.

DESSERTS

BREAD AND BUTTER PUDDING

Less than 25 minutes

A retro heart-warming dessert that makes great use of bread. The sweetness of sultanas, the richness of custard and the crunch of sweet baked bread—heavenly!

INGREDIENTS

40 g (2 tbsp) or a snack-sized box of sultanas (golden raisins) or raisins

15 ml (1 tbsp) butter, plus extra for greasing the dish

1 slice white (or soft brown) bread

1 egg

2 tbsp sour cream or plain double (thick) cream, if you have it

2 tsp caster (superfine) sugar

4–5 drops vanilla extract

PREPARATION

Preheat the oven to 190°C/375°F/Gas mark 5.

In a heatproof bowl, soak the raisins in some boiling water until softened, about 5 minutes.

Grease a 10 cm (4 in) diameter ramekin with butter.

Spread the remaining butter over the slice of bread, taking care to cover it right up to the corners. Cut the bread into 12 squares.

In a small bowl, mix together the egg, cream, sugar and vanilla.

Roughly layer about half of the bread pieces over the base of the ramekin, then scatter over about half of the raisins. Repeat with another layer of bread and the rest of the raisins.

Gently pour over the egg mixture, taking care to soak all of the top pieces of bread with the mixture.

Bake for about 20 minutes, or until golden brown. Serve hot.

CARAMELISED APPLES

20 minutes | Freezes well and makes a double portion

A classic interpretation of apples which combines their sweetness with a buttery caramel sauce.

SERVING SUGGESTION   Great as a dessert, but also works beautifully served with a pork chop, as an apple sauce

INGREDIENTS

3 apples, peeled and halved and core removed (you can use practically any kind except Granny Smith)
1 tbsp butter
3 tbsp brown tightly packed sugar
3 tbsp white wine (or water)
Vanilla ice-cream, to serve

OPTIONAL INGREDIENTS

Prunes or sultanas (golden raisins), if you have any.

PREPARATION

Cut each apple half into 6–8 segments.

Melt the butter in a non-stick pan over a medium-low heat, add the apple segments, then sprinkle over the brown sugar. Stir to ensure the sugar melts and doesn't stick. Cover and cook for 5–6 minutes fairly slowly.

Remove the lid, pour in the little white wine, and allow to cook for about 5 minutes with the lid off. Stir gently with a spatula. The aim is to ensure the apple segments are soft and that the juices escape and mix with the butter, sugar and wine.

Serve warm with ice-cream.

INDIVIDUAL CRÈME CARAMEL

30 minutes, plus cooling time

The cornerstone of French desserts! Delicious baked custard swimming in its own caramel.

INGREDIENTS

FOR THE CARAMEL

1 tbsp caster (superfine) sugar

5 tbsp water

FOR THE CUSTARD

1 egg

3 tbsp milk or cream

2 tsp caster (superfine) sugar

Dash of vanilla extract (optional)

PREPARATION

Preheat the oven to 180°C (350°F/Gas mark 4).

For the caramel, put the sugar and water in a small pan. Place over a medium heat and swirl a couple of times to dissolve the sugar. Boil slowly until large bubbles appear and it starts to turn a caramel colour, roughly 5 minutes. Watch it carefully as it will turn dark brown very quickly (you want it to be a honey tone). Pour the caramel into the bottom of an 8 cm (3 in) diameter ramekin.

In a separate mixing bowl, whisk the egg, milk or cream, sugar and vanilla together so that all the egg is incorporated.

Pour the custard on top of the caramel in the ramekin.

Place the ramekin into a larger baking dish with sides and pour about 500 ml (17 fl oz/generous 2 cups) boiling water into the baking dish so that it comes about half way up the outside of the ramekin.

Cover the entire baking dish with foil and place on the middle rack in the oven. Bake for 20-25 minutes, or until set.

Remove from the oven and run a knife around the custard to help release it from the ramekin. Place a serving plate on top of the ramekin and then turn the plate and ramekin over (carefully) so that the ramekin is now on top of the plate. Hold both and give them a shake, then lift up the ramekin.

The crème caramel should slide out onto the plate, with its caramel sauce all around. Enjoy warm.

MINI CHOCOLATE AND JAM POT

Less than 25 minutes

This dessert is a little pot of sophistication, yet is easy to make. The baked chocolate custard delights, with a shock of cherry jam at its heart.

INGREDIENTS
50 g (1¾ oz) dark (bittersweet) chocolate
1 tsp caster (superfine) sugar
1 egg
1 tbsp milk or cream
1 tsp cherry or your favourite jam (optional)

PREPARATION
Preheat the oven to 180°C/350°F/Gas mark 4.

Melt the chocolate in heatproof bowl either in the microwave or set over a pan of gently simmering water.

Add the sugar to the chocolate and stir to combine.

Add the egg and the milk or cream. Stir until well combined and the mixture is glossy.

Place the cherry jam in an 8 cm (3 in) diameter ramekin. Pour over the chocolate mixture leaving a 2–3 cm (1 in) gap at the top for the chocolate custard to rise.

Place the ramekin into a larger baking dish with sides and pour boiling water into the baking dish so that it comes about half way up the outside of the ramekin.

Cover the entire baking dish with foil and place on the middle rack in the oven. Bake for 30 minutes, or until the pudding set.

Remove the ramekin from the oven and carefully remove the foil (there will be some steam trapped underneath)

Leave to cool for a few minutes and then enjoy. Serve warm.

CHOCOLATE CAKE

30 minutes, plus cooling time

A cute little cake for one with a delectable icing to cap it off.

INGREDIENTS

1 tbsp butter, plus extra for greasing
3 tbsp caster (superfine) sugar
1 egg
55 g (2 oz/¼ cup) self-raising (self-rising) flour
1 tbsp unsweetened cocoa powder
1 tbsp milk

FOR THE ICING

2 tbsp sour cream or double (thick/heavy) cream
1 tbsp caster (superfine) sugar
2 tbsp Milo (or other drinking chocolate)

PREPARATION

Preheat the oven to 180°C/350°F/Gas mark 4.

Grease a 10 cm (4 in) diameter ramekin with butter.

Melt the butter in a pan over gentle heat or in the microwave in a suitable bowl. Stir in the sugar whisking together for 2-3 minutes or until most of the sugar has dissolved. Stir in the egg.

Sift over the flour and cocoa powder and stir to combine. Add the milk and stir again.

Pour the batter into the ramekin and bake for 20 minutes. When the cake is cooled, it should be pulling away from the sides of the ramekin slightly and spring back lightly when touched. Set aside for 5 minutes before turning out onto a wire rack, turn upright and leave to cool.

Meanwhile, prepare the icing by combining the cream and sugar, then adding the milo and stirring well.

Spread the icing over the cooled cake and serve.

FRUIT CRUMBLE

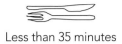

Less than 35 minutes

This fruit crumble is so easy to put together, most of the time is in the baking! It is delicious cold, too, served with yoghurt as a breakfast alternative.

INGREDIENTS

1 tbsp melted butter, plus extra for greasing
1 dessert apple or 1 cup (140 g/4¾ oz) mixed berries (fresh or frozen) or a combination
3 tbsp rolled oats
1 tbsp brown sugar (tightly packed or light)
¼ tsp cinnamon
Cream, to serve (sour cream works as an accompaniment here)

EXTRA OPTIONAL INGREDIENTS AND VARIATION

A couple of tablespoons of sultanas (golden raisins) for extra colour and flavour
Swap the apple/berries for pear, peach or prunes, if you prefer.

PREPARATION

Preheat the oven to 190°C/375°F/Gas mark 5.

Grease a 10 cm (4 in) ramekin with butter.

Peel and core the apple and then cut into very small dice. Place these dice into the base of the ramekin. Mix in any other fruit you are using.

In a small mixing bowl, combine the melted butter, oats, sugar and cinnamon.

Sprinkle the oat mixture evenly over the top of the fruit and bake for 30 minutes, or until golden brown on top.

Serve hot with cream.

LIL' APPLE CAKE

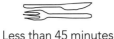

Less than 45 minutes

Lovely to nibble on over a few days (best kept wrapped in plastic wrap) or to make when a friend is popping over.

INGREDIENTS

1 sweet apple (Gala is a good variety to use)
55 g (2 oz/¼ cup) caster (superfine) sugar
1 egg
Few drops of vanilla extract
Dash of brandy or rum (optional)
115 g (4 oz/½ cup) self-raising (self-rising) flour
1 tablespoon milk
50 g (1¾ oz) unsalted butter, melted, plus extra for greasing

PREPARATION

Preheat the oven to 180°C (350°F/Gas mark 4) and grease a small 10 cm (4 in) cake tin (pan)—even if it's non-stick, grease it.

Peel and core the apple and cut into quarters. Cut each quarter into thin slices, ideally 6–8 slices per quarter.

Whisk the sugar and egg together. Add the vanilla and brandy or rum (if using).

Slowly add the flour, milk and melted butter until all are incorporated and there are no lumps.

Stir in the apple slices so they are coated with the batter, but be careful not to break the slices.

Pour the mixture into the prepared tin and bake for 30–35 minutes. When the cake is cooled, it should be golden, have pulled away from the sides of the tin, and spring back slightly when pressed in the centre.

Leave to cool slightly before running a knife around the edge of the cake and turning out on to a serving place. Turn right way up and serve.

GINGER-BAKED PEARS

Less than 35 minutes

Pear and ginger form such a lasting, complementary relationship, don't they? This dessert lets each of them shine.

INGREDIENTS

Butter, for greasing

1 large pear

1 egg

2 tbsp mascarpone, ricotta or double (thick/heavy) cream

1 tbsp caster (superfine) sugar

1 tsp grated ginger (fresh or from a jar)

PREPARATION

Preheat the oven to 190°C/375°F/Gas mark 5.

Grease a 10 cm (4 in) diameter ramekin with butter.

Peel and core the pear and then cut into slices about 5 mm (¼ in) thick.

Line the base of the ramekin with the pear slices.

In a small bowl, mix together the egg, mascarpone, sugar and ginger.

Pour the egg mixture over the pear slices and then bake for about 20 minutes, or until the custard is set and golden on top. Serve hot.

THE MATRIX (PART 1)

	Stracciatella	Slimmers soup	Summer chikcen salad	Ham salad	Chicken and couscous salad	Veggie couscous	Mushroom omelette	Quick fritatta	Salmon-baked Eggs	Creamy Bacon Pizza	Vegetarian Pizza	Salami Pizza	Tomato and Bacon Gnocchi	Spinach and Chicken Gnocci	Creamy Salmon Gnocci	Pasta Carbonara	Mushroom Risotto	Chicken Risotto	Garlicky Pasta	Pasta Salad
...tter (Butter)						Δ	Δ	Δ	Δ								Δ	Δ	Δ	
...aby spinach or rocket	Δ	Δ		Δ	Δ	Δ			Δ		Δ	Δ	Δ	Δ	Δ		Δ	Δ		
...by cos			Δ	Δ	Δ															
...rrots (fresh)		Δ		Δ	Δ	Δ														
...erry tomatoes				Δ	Δ							Δ	Δ			Δ				Δ
...ur cream (Sour cream)										Δ				Δ	Δ	Δ	Δ	Δ		
...eese (grated mixed)	Δ			Δ			Δ	Δ	Δ	Δ	Δ	Δ	Δ	Δ	Δ	Δ			Δ	
...eese (processed)						Δ	Δ	Δ	Δ			Δ	Δ	Δ	Δ	Δ				
...eese (marinated)				Δ	Δ	Δ	Δ				Δ	Δ					Δ	Δ		Δ
...uscous (Couscous)					Δ	Δ														
...gs (Eggs)	Δ			Δ			Δ	Δ	Δ							Δ				
...halots (Shalots)			Δ	Δ	Δ	Δ	Δ	Δ		Δ	Δ	Δ	Δ	Δ	Δ	Δ	Δ	Δ		Δ
...occhi (Gnocchi)	Δ	Δ											Δ	Δ	Δ					
...mons and lemon juice	Δ	Δ	Δ	Δ	Δ	Δ														
...yonnaise (Mayonnaise)				Δ																
...edy mustard				Δ																
...on mustard (Dijon mustard)				Δ																
...zen pastry (frozen pastry)										Δ	Δ	Δ								
...t (new) potatoes				Δ																
...pared mixed vegetables (eslaw mix)		Δ		Δ																
...pared mixed vegetables (zen vegetables)	Δ	Δ				Δ		Δ							Δ					
...za-base sauce (Pizza-base sauce)										Δ	Δ	Δ	Δ	Δ	Δ	Δ				
...ns pulses (beans pulses)		Δ		Δ	Δ	Δ														Δ
...dy-made stock (ready-made stock)	Δ	Δ															Δ	Δ	Δ	
...oked or cured meat ...h as ham, bacon, chicken			Δ	Δ	Δ		Δ	Δ	Δ	Δ	Δ	Δ	Δ	Δ	Δ	Δ				
...s tuna, salmon, ...omeat				Δ																

THE MATRIX (PART 2)

	Steak Dinner for One	Classic Fish Pouch	Asian Fish Pouch	Salmon Teriyaki with Pea Mash	Tuna and Bean Bake	Quick Spaghetti and Meatballs	Mama's Lemon Chicken	Easy Stir-fry	Get your Greens Stir-fry	Quick Katsu Dan	Solo Stroganoff	Quick Lamb Casserole	Gourmet BLT	Potato and Leek Soup	Leftover Vegetable Soup	Bolognese Sauce	Ratatouille	Spicy Red Beans	Baked Dinner for One	Shepherd's Pie
Butter	Δ	Δ		Δ	Δ		Δ				Δ			Δ	Δ					Δ
Baby spinach or rocket	Δ	Δ	Δ		Δ	Δ	Δ	Δ	Δ			Δ	Δ	Δ						
Baby cos													Δ							
Carrots (fresh)			Δ				Δ					Δ			Δ	Δ			Δ	
Cherry tomatoes						Δ							Δ		Δ	Δ	Δ	Δ		
Sour cream	Δ				Δ	Δ					Δ	Δ		Δ				Δ	Δ	
Cheese (grated mixed)					Δ	Δ												Δ		Δ
Cheese (processed)	Δ				Δ	Δ	Δ							Δ						
Cheese (marinated)						Δ														
Couscous																				
Eggs	Δ									Δ										
Eschalots	Δ			Δ	Δ		Δ				Δ	Δ	Δ		Δ	Δ	Δ	Δ	Δ	
Gnocchi																				
Lemons and lemon juice	Δ	Δ	Δ				Δ	Δ			Δ		Δ		Δ	Δ				
Mayonnaise										Δ			Δ							
Seedy mustard	Δ																			
Dijon mustard	Δ																			
Frozen pastry																				
Chat (new) potatoes	Δ													Δ						
Prepared mixed vegetables (coleslaw mix)	Δ		Δ					Δ		Δ					Δ					
Prepared mixed vegetables (frozen vegetables)	Δ						Δ	Δ				Δ								
Pizza-base sauce						Δ										Δ	Δ			
Cans pulses					Δ							Δ			Δ			Δ		
Ready-made stock											Δ	Δ		Δ	Δ			Δ		
Smoked or cured meat such as ham, bacon, chicken						Δ								Δ	Δ	Δ			Δ	
Cans tuna, salmon, crabmeat					Δ														Δ	

	Nachos for One	Savoury Scrolls	Jack of Spuds	Fragrant Lamb Chops	Quick Beef Goulash	Provencale Chicken	Minestrone Soup	Pasta Primavera	Leftover Lamb Curry	French-style Lentils	Fried Rice	Green Salad	Tomato Salad	Trio Salad	Cucumber Salad	French Beans	Mashed Potato	Sautéed Mushrooms	Classic Coleslaw	Easy Mixed Vegetables	Lemon Vegetables	Quick Potato Salad	Squashed Spuds
...ter																△	△	△		△			
...by spinach or rocket	△	△	△			△	△	△	△	△				△			△					△	
...y Cos												△											
...rots (fresh)	△					△	△	△	△	△				△					△		△		
...rry tomatoes	△				△	△	△	△					△	△								△	
...r cream	△		△	△			△								△		△	△				△	
...ese (grated mixed)	△	△	△					△						△					△				
...ese (processed)		△						△									△						
...ese (marinated)	△							△						△									
...scous																							
...s												△										△	
...halots	△				△	△	△	△	△	△		△	△	△		△	△	△	△			△	
...cchi																							
...ons and lemon juice				△			△		△	△					△		△	△	△	△	△		
...onnaise																			△			△	
...dy mustard																							
...n mustard																							
...en pastry		△																					
...(new) potatoes																						△	△
...ared mixed vegetables (...eslaw mix)	△						△	△	△										△	△			
...ared mixed vegetables (...en vegetables)							△	△	△		△												
...a-base sauce		△			△	△	△	△															
...s pulses			△				△	△	△	△	△					△							
...ly-made stock					△	△			△														
...ked or cured meat such as ham, ...n, chicken		△					△		△	△												△	
...tuna, salmon, crabmeat																							

INDEX

About the Authors

Catherine Baker and Diana Ferguson are sisters. They have designed and taught cooking programs for their local community college for the past 10 years. Both are passionate about good food and enjoy sharing their knowledge and know-how with others. Their 'Cooking for One' workshops and talks have drawn sell-out crowds, not only because they offer practical advice, but the feedback suggests that attendees have found the recipes delicious and easy to make.

Diana is the creative brains behind the recipes and Catherine likes to write. So, while they each achieved qualifications in catering, hospitality and training, they know that their real strength lies in their teamwork and designing recipes together that actually work.

The girls have spent years working in kitchens, getting to know the tastebuds and minds of their customers and all the while discovering what flavours people enjoy, and understanding what really motivates them to cook. The end result is no-fuss, tasty dishes that are easily achievable by the single home cook. This book contains just a sample of their best recipes. Enjoy!